Praise for
People First Leadership

An insightful and original exploration of company culture, and the critical importance of inspiring emotions to spur engagement—and results. An essential read for any leader who understands that people are what make businesses live or die.

—**Jack Welch,** Former CEO of General Electric

In *People First Leadership*, Eduardo Braun shows how managing people's hearts and minds plays a fundamental role in every aspect of effective, results-oriented leadership— from the necessity of making tough choices and the importance of a strong vision for the future to creating a culture of curiosity and innovation. This is essential reading for any manager.

—**Robert J. Herbold,** Chief Operating Officer
(retired), Microsoft Corporation

As a past HSM speaker, I met most of the high-profile leaders mentioned in this book. I even had a friendly debate with Jack Welch. Ed Braun's questions during his interviews with me were always excellent. This book on the soft factors of emotion and culture that great leaders manifest is long overdue.

—**Philip Kotler,** bestselling author of *Kotler on Marketing*
and S. C. Johnson Distinguished Professor of International
Marketing at Northwestern University

Edward Braun has explored success and leadership in this book derived from his series of Business Forums. As a man with six children I've always considered him one of the richest men I know—but aside from this good fortune, there are many good ideas and lessons to be learned from him.

—**Francis Ford Coppola,** screenwriter, film director, and producer

People First Leadership is an insightful book that provides a remarkably clear and practical teaching for any leader who wants to pursue excellence by developing a successful culture that speaks to the heart of their people. Definitively challenging.

— **Álvaro Uribe Vélez,** Former President of Colombia

As we have moved from the Industrial Age to the Information Age, increasingly we are recognizing that data is not knowledge, never mind wisdom. With that in mind, success increasingly will come to those with high degrees of EQ. Drawing on the words of scores of leaders he has interviewed and his own insights, Braun boldly redefines the role of CEO as Chief Emotions Officer. His book is especially clear and relevant, not just to businesspeople, but to anyone who wants to effect change.

—**Christie Hefner,** Former CEO and
Chairman, Playboy Enterprises

A must-read for anyone looking to learn unique leadership lessons from the minds of the world's greatest leaders. Eduardo gives us personal and direct access to their mindsets and to their leadership journeys. For leaders across all cultures the message is clear—high-performance leadership must include awareness of emotions to execute a successful strategy. Eduardo's message is clear—leadership is personal.

—**George Kohlrieser,** IMD Professor of Leadership and
Organizational Behavior, author of *Hostage at the Table*

A well-told story delivers a meaningful emotional experience, equally impacting both head and heart. Eduardo Braun's insightful new book, *People First Leadership*, demonstrates how striking this same balance in business and government empowers humanistic leadership. Bravo Eduardo!

—**Robert McKee,** author of *Story*

Eduardo Braun is a masterful conversationalist turned storyteller. *People First Leadership* rightly focuses business action on emotion and its many dimensions, drawing wisdom from the good and great of business to illuminate the pathway to winning.

—**Kevin Roberts,** Chairman Saatchi & Saatchi,
Head Coach Publicis Groupe

I have been interviewed many times in the last forty years. Without any doubt, one of the most compelling, interesting, and in-depth interviews that I have done was made by Eduardo Braun. His expertise in this field is undeniable, and he has been blessed with a very personal and candid approach to access deep into each one of his partners on so many worldwide events. This book is a wonderful way of absorbing the talent, leadership, experience, and success of great men, through the now great writing of the best interviewer in the world.

  —Nando Parrado, survivor of the 1972 plane crash in the Chilean
    mountains and bestselling author of *Miracle in the Andes*

This is a complete and successful undertaking, nicely integrating the key roles leadership plays in determining organizational success. Particularly interesting and effective is the book's treatment of how "hard" factors affecting performance (e.g., strategy) are interdependent with critical "soft" factors, such as culture and emotion, and how these soft factors can multiply and intensify desired leadership results. This is an effective treatise of leadership as a complex phenomenon that should be on every manager's bookshelf.

  —Lawrence Hrebiniak, Emeritus Professor of
    Strategic Management, Wharton School

People First Leadership brings together the best minds in business to make a counterintuitive—yet powerful—case for the importance of emotion in organizational success. By adopting the five key roles of Braun's proposed "Chief Emotions Officer," you can use the softer side of management to transform your own organization.

  —Daniel H. Pink, *New York Times* bestselling
    author of *Drive* and *A Whole New Mind*

Over the years I've seen Eduardo interview heads of state, heads of corporations, and global thought leaders. He has now skillfully extracted the leadership lessons and shared them in *People First Leadership*, showing what the best leaders actually do, and the crucial role that emotions play in changing behavior.

  —Renée Mauborgne, INSEAD Professor and coauthor
    of the global bestseller *Blue Ocean Strategy*

Eduardo Braun's book beautifully portrays why the "intangibles" are more motivating than the "tangible" in creating a dynamic, people-focused organizational culture, which leads to personal fulfillment for employees; an energizing *esprit de corps* for all participants; and mesmerizing results for the entity. Eduardo's book is a bible for those leaders who aspire to inspire.

—**Herb Kelleher,** Cofounder, Chairman Emeritus,
and Former CEO of Southwest Airlines

In *People First Leadership*, Eduardo Braun puts the focus squarely where it belongs: on helping individuals at work develop their innate potential. In the battle to overcome the disengagement and underperformance that plagues economies around the world, Braun offers a practical tool kit for unleashing the creativity, passion, and commitment that drives high performance.

—**Gary Hamel,** author of *The Future of Management*
and *What Matters Now*

I've known Eduardo for many years, and I've always admired his deep understanding of what really drives people. *People First Leadership* is sure to change how you think about getting the best out of yourself, your team, and your organization.

—**Rudy Giuliani,** former mayor of New York City

From my perspective, Eduardo Braun has captured two of the essential lessons of leadership. First, it's mostly a people game. And second, if you hire great people and build a great organisational culture, everything else seems to take care of itself.

—**John Sadowsky,** author of *The Seven Rules of Storytelling*

PEOPLE
F1RST
LEADERSHIP

HOW THE BEST LEADERS USE
CULTURE AND EMOTION TO DRIVE
UNPRECEDENTED RESULTS

EDUARDO P. BRAUN

New York   Chicago   San Francisco   Athens   London   Madrid
Mexico City   Milan   New Delhi   Singapore   Sydney   Toronto

1 2 3 4 5 6 7 8 9 0   DOC   21 20 19 18 17 16

ISBN   978-1-259-83540-7
MHID   1-259-83540-5

e-ISBN   978-1-259-83541-4
e-MHID   1-259-83541-3

Library of Congress Cataloging-in-Publication Data

Names: Braun, Eduardo P., author.
Title: People first leadership: how the best leaders use culture and emotion to drive
    unprecedented results / by Eduardo P. Braun.
Description: 1 Edition. | New York : McGraw-Hill Education, 2016.
Identifiers: LCCN 2016024452 (print) | LCCN 2016027255 (ebook) | ISBN
    9781259835407 (hardback : alk. paper) | ISBN 1259835405 (alk. paper) |
    ISBN 9781259835414 () | ISBN 1259835413 ()
Subjects: LCSH: Leadership. | BISAC: BUSINESS & ECONOMICS / Leadership.
Classification: LCC HM1261 .B753 2016 (print) | LCC HM1261 (ebook) |
    DDC 303.3/4—dc23
LC record available at https://lccn.loc.gov/2016024452

McGraw-Hill Education books are available at special quantity discounts to use as premiums and sales promotions or for use in corporate training programs. To contact a representative, please visit the Contact Us pages at www.mhprofessional.com.

*To all those who labor passionately to make their dreams real,
among them, my six children, Delfina, Eduardo, Mateo,
Felipe, Jaime, and Teresita, and my wife, Alejandra.*

CONTENTS

Foreword

In this invaluable book, Eduardo Braun has put together a very practical framework for personal and organizational leadership development and for fostering a healthy culture, which—as he so clearly points out—has these days become the ultimate source of competitive advantage by allowing organizations to attract the best people, helping that talent become better each day, and inspiring them to passionately give their collective best.

In line with his own truly global perspective and humble personality, Eduardo does not try to force on us a rigid, one-size-fits-all framework or approach for our personal or organizational transformation. Rather, he presents us with a myriad of fascinating testimonies from various leaders with very different life stories and passions so that we react to what truly ignites our own passions and ambitions. Despite the fact that I have heard and even interacted with several of these leaders many times, I was amazed by the extraordinary collection of invaluable stories and quotes Eduardo has been able to gather and select for us from thousands of hours of his privileged conversations.

I first met Eduardo some 20 years ago when, as a search consultant, I interviewed him as a potential candidate. I was immediately taken by his combination of insatiable curiosity, contagious enthusiasm, and deep personal humility.

More recently, I have had numerous opportunities to engage with him as a public speaker, when the roles were reversed and he interviewed me for different global events and TV shows. I have really come to admire Eduardo's unique style. He really enjoys what he does, and in addition to his amazing curiosity and brilliant insight, he is always looking for the most practical applications of our research and life lessons, particularly regarding the best ways to lead our organizations and, perhaps more important, the best ways to lead ourselves.

Because of my profession, I have also been lucky to know, interact with, and follow hundreds of the best global leaders from all walks of life, and I realize how much they have inspired and helped me professionally and personally. Like Eduardo, I am convinced that by examining their life lessons we can all become much better leaders and foster the type of culture that simultaneously makes people happy and strongly multiplies results.

We are living in times of unprecedented volatility, uncertainty, complexity, and ambiguity, when, in order to prosper and even survive, organizational and personal reinvention is no longer an option, but an urgent need. This book could not be more relevant and timely as an invaluable resource for reinvention by inspiring us with the best and enabling us to follow some of their truly unique pearls of wisdom to become much better people and leaders each day.

—**Claudio Fernández-Aráoz**
Senior Adviser of Egon Zehnder,
author of *Great People Decisions*

Prologue

In June 2005, I was having a drink on the terrace of the Four Seasons Hotel in Mexico City with Jack and Suzy Welch, hoping to get to know them a bit. The following day I was scheduled to talk onstage with Jack before a crowd of 2,000 people about how to succeed as a leader at a major event for managers and business people at the impressive Hippodrome of the Americas in Mexico City. As director of the HSM Group, the global multimedia management company that started Expomanagement and the World Business Forum, it was my pleasure and honor to travel the globe interviewing the world's most prominent players and renowned experts in business and politics on the topics of leadership and management—people like Jack Welch.

In the past, these interviews had consisted of the "big name" speaking for an hour and then me asking questions for 20 or 30 minutes. The next day, however, I was going to try something new: Jack and I were going to have a 90-minute conversation onstage. This was a bit of a challenge and, beyond offering sincere hospitality to him and his wife, I hoped that getting to know Jack better before we were under the lights would help better prepare me for the next day's Q&A. We talked about life, swapped leadership stories, and discussed business opportunities. I found them both thoroughly charming and began to look forward to the following day's interview.

I had thoroughly prepared and, when I arrived at the conference hall the next day, I had several pages of notes and questions to support me. A few minutes before starting the session, I gave my folder to a colleague while I took a moment to ready myself and to go to the restroom. When I came back, she had lost the folder! I was totally desperate about having to walk onstage with nothing but empty white sheets of paper!

How did I get into that predicament, standing backstage holding a bundle of blank paper, waiting to conduct a public interview with the former chairman and CEO of General Electric—the man who raised GE's value 4,000 percent during his 20-year tenure, from $14 billion to roughly $400 billion[1]—in front of an audience of accomplished leaders that included folks like Rudy Giuliani and former CMO of the Coca Cola Company Peter Sealey?

I was originally trained as an industrial engineer. When I graduated from the University of Buenos Aires, my biggest dream was to do an MBA at the Wharton School so that I could gain the expertise necessary to manage my family's business.

As so often happens, however, circumstances change and we must change with them. After graduating from Wharton, I worked for Booz Allen and Hamilton in Paris, eventually returning to Argentina and starting Management & Investment Group, my own strategy consulting boutique. In early 1999, I joined the executive management team of the HSM Group and, over the next dozen years, helped produce events in New York, Chicago, Los Angeles, Frankfurt, Milan, Madrid, Mexico, and Buenos Aires. These events included multiple keynote speakers, all of whom were among the most recognizable leaders on the world stage or the most renowned in their fields. To name just a few: Bill Clinton, Tony Blair, Mikhail Gorbachev, Madeleine Albright, Colin Powell, Peter Drucker, Michael Porter, Daniel Goleman, Rudy Giuliani, Carlos Brito, George Lucas, Michael Eisner, Herb Kelleher, Tony Hsieh, Carly Fiorina, Philip Kotler, Nando Parrado, Stephen Covey and, of course, Jack Welch. We offered audiences a chance to hear these exceptional people in a format uniquely designed for learning and inspiration. From all over Europe, Latin America and the United States, business people came to our events and were transformed by the experience we provided.

That's why I was standing backstage waiting to go on with Jack, nervously fumbling blank papers and trying to remember what I had planned to ask!

Once the conversation began, the only thing I could do was to concentrate deeply and constantly think things like "Could I apply what Jack is saying in my team and company?" "What about the average person in the audience? What additional information would he need to apply these concepts in his organization?" "Don't just share concepts! Give me examples!"

This attitude, rather than following prewritten questions, turned out to be the secret to what was one of my best interviews ever—even according to Jack, who warmly congratulated me. Having taught me the virtue of really enjoying the exchange, this experience helped me to grow significantly as an interviewer.

But perhaps even more important was what Jack said during the interview. In contrast to many business experts, who spent considerable time stressing the importance of strategy and planning to achievement, Jack's prescriptions for success as an executive or businessperson were mostly about people, values, and differentiation, and very little about strategy. That really surprised me. In fact, Jack's messages about strategy were relatively plain and simple: You need to find the "aha" in your business, and it is better if you are number one or two in your markets. Period. What was revelatory was where he actually saw the key to successful leadership. What was really important, he explained, was how you treated people, having the best and smartest on your teams, selecting a few key values and behaviors, and being candid!

I was surprised by this message. Though there was a cohort of people who had said somewhat similar things before—for instance, Peter Drucker, who, beginning with his 1954 book *The Practice of Management*, promoted a leadership style where strategic objectives went hand in hand with people's personal objectives and business issues were treated through a humanistic perspective—this sincere focus on people, values, and behaviors was very different from what I usually heard and read about in terms of business leadership and management and wasn't at all what one usually saw in the business world, where strategy was king. Indeed, for decades, strategy was the only ball game.

We can see this trend's infancy in the early years of the twentieth century. In 1911, Frederick Winslow Taylor announced his four principles of "scientific management," all of which focused on the definition, supervision, and execution of well-defined tasks.[2] Five years later, French-born Henri Fayol published an influential book in which he argued that management had only six functions: forecasting, planning, organizing, commanding, coordinating, and controlling. Booz Allen & Hamilton, the management consulting firm for which I would work 75 years later, first opened its doors in the midst of this movement toward strategy, in 1914.

It was, however, in the 1960s and '70s that what we now recognize as the obsession with strategy really took shape, starting with Bruce Henderson's departure in the early sixties from the original management consulting firm Arthur D. Little (founded 1886) to create the Boston Consulting Group. When he invented the "BCG

Growth-Share Matrix" in 1970, Henderson popularized the concepts of portfolio analysis and strategic management and revolutionized the industry. The BCG Growth Matrix is a framework to evaluate the strategic position of a business brand portfolio and its potential. It classifies business portfolios into four categories based on industry attractiveness (growth rate of that industry) and competitive position (relative market share). These categories are characterized as stars, question marks, cash cows, and dogs, but there is no place for people. That didn't stop it from becoming the go-to analysis tool for decades. The success of BCG gave birth to new "strategy consulting" firms like Bain & Company, Strategic Planning Associates, Braxton Associates, LEK Partnership, and Monitor Company, the latter of which was founded by Michael Porter, author of *Competitive Strategy*, published in 1980 and the first of several books on strategy considered to be the foundation of the field.

In one of the interviews I did with Michael Porter, he reiterated his history-making "five forces framework," where he defines strategy as follows: ***"Strategy is finding a different way to compete, to create a different sort of value for the customer which allows the company to prosper, to achieve sustainable profitability"***—in other words, the "combination of the ends for which the firm is striving and the means by which it is seeking to get there."[3] We could also call this paradigm that makes strategy a central tenet the "business-as-usual" model. In this model, the CEO and his team perform different tasks that together make up the value chain:

- They design a strategy based on a unique form of competing (differentiation) in order to reach out to a particular segment of the market with a value proposition.

- They manufacture or deliver a product or service, which is the foundation of their value proposition; this product or service has a price and a marketing and sales plan.

- They define the procedures and job descriptions necessary to accomplish the products and services, and then build a team of people and organize it according to each person's expertise, thus creating a variety of departments, such as *marketing, finance, engineering, production*, and *human resources*.

The final delivery of the value proposition is only possible because of this basic design, starting with the appropriate strategy. Strategy is your unique way of competing in a market.

Indeed, the key to Porter's definition of strategy is the understanding of "how a business is going to compete." Typically, strategy encompasses how a company defines all its business variables: its products, prices, costs, operations, blueprint, and so on. Some of the generic strategies are, for example, "being a low-cost producer" or a "differentiated product/service provider." In the first case, a company sets all the business variables so that it minimizes overall costs, which allows it to compete on price. So, from product design to engineering and manufacturing, everything is focused on lowering costs. On the contrary, when a company chooses a differentiated strategy, it adds features that are unique and valued by the customers so that they are chosen over competing products and services.

This historical focus on strategy meant that, from the late seventies until only recently, the main terms through which a business was analyzed were its hard variables—therefore, significant research and attention has primarily been devoted only to the framework and underlying variables of strategy.

Strategy is undoubtedly an important part of management, and more often than not, it's the main focus of the board of directors. Maybe that's a result of Porter's influence and the dominance of his "five forces framework," which took the business world by storm when it was introduced over 35 years ago. Maybe it has to do with famous strategic consulting firms such as BCG, McKinsey, Booz Allen, and Bain, organizations that have pushed tens of thousands of professionals toward strategy. Or maybe it's all just the consequence of a long history of focusing on production strategies and the management of resources stretching back to the dawn of the Industrial Revolution. Whatever the cause, strategy has long been the leading doctrine in business management and executive education.

But it was perhaps an exaggeration to say earlier that strategy was the only game in town. In 1977, Peter Drucker published *People and Performance: The Best of Peter Drucker on Management*, bringing to the fore his belief that "people are an organization's most valuable resource, and that a manager's job is both to prepare people to perform and give them freedom to do so."[4] Drucker's stress on the primacy of people as the most valuable resource played a significant role in the evolution of human resources, as companies struggled to understand the deeper motivations of their employees and to plumb the depths of how human beings work in the context of organizations and jobs. In fact, even during the eighties and nineties, when strategy was undoubtedly the biggest game in town, particularly for CEOs, there was significant work done in the fields of organizational behavior, organizational culture, and the management of people at work.

The field of psychology lends us another way of thinking about the predominant historical focus on strategy. The "selective attention" test demonstrates that the way we perceive reality is shaped in large part by the question we are trying to answer. The test starts with a question: "How many times do the players wearing white T-shirts pass the basketball?" Then, participants watch a video in which two teams pass a basketball, counting only the passes made by the team in white. In their quest to accurately count the number of passes, many people finish the video without realizing that, about halfway through, a person dressed in a gorilla suit walks into the frame and starts dancing in the middle of the court.[5] The same phenomenon occurs in the field of leadership. We are always going back to the same questions: "What is our strategy?" or "What is our competitive advantage?" We are so focused on those issues that many gorillas stroll by without us even noticing.

That is what happened to me throughout my career as an executive. When I first began working as a strategic consultant, I never thought about culture, mood, state of mind, or emotion affecting a person's or team's ability to perform. With my engineering degree and MBA, I felt I had the necessary tools to analyze how companies are designed and how they execute their strategy and business plans.

I had been brought up in and still belonged to a school of thought that relied solely on the "hard" variables of numbers, strategy, and business design. I ignored people-centric "soft" variables, assuming that their "softness" somehow made them less important and easier to manage. Having accepted these principles as a given, I was under the impression that the only thing an organization needed in order to make sure the "people part" worked well was a set of assertive managers. I pushed aside any other theories that might get in the way of such a straightforward approach.

Actually, it is not that matters related to people were unimportant, but they had a very different place in the overall thinking about business than the one I will ultimately present in this book. The general consensus in the business world was that, though variables that relate to the heart and soul of human beings were hypothetically important, there simply was no place for them in the traditional strategy models. Labor was considered a "factor of production" and as such the focus was on its economic productivity. As a result, all the topics related to employees were supposed to be addressed with an exclusive focus on productivity. They were considered "human resources," and all management techniques like training, process improvement, compensation and incentive plans, motivation, and teamwork, among many others, were focused on productivity. Employees were a factor of production needed to implement a given strategy, but they were not a key to business success on their own.

I was so convinced of the importance of hard variables that I stood by my convictions even in my first years of interviewing esteemed leaders. It was only after I had been conducting interviews for several years that I was able to let go of my preconceived notion that management was all about strategy. That's when I really started to pay attention and truly listen to the stories that these notable figures were telling, leaving aside the bias and value judgments that had constrained me in the past. And that was really caused by the growing frequency with which I was hearing something other than strategy play the primary role in ideas of successful leadership. That transition marks the moment when I began to discover a new reality, one that revealed to me that the key to good performance is to manage people's hearts and minds.

Onstage with Jack Welch, I had my first vision of the gorilla in the room when he began talking about the importance of people, behavior, and values. Interestingly, as I traveled all over the globe speaking with leaders, I began to hear sentiments similar to his over and over again. Although a few people were researching and writing about this, it was still far from mainstream, and I would have been hard-pressed to find anyone actually putting these ideas into practice in a business. But that was also what was so exciting, so revelatory to me: learning what was outside the mainstream at the time and slowly seeing it seep in. As I opened myself to asking different questions, I actually began to see a different reality, a different focus for successful business leadership. For, indeed, a focus on people or what I would call culture rather than strategy is what I kept hearing from leader after leader: people and culture!

For instance, in 2008 I interviewed Zappos CEO Tony Hsieh for the talk show I had on the 24-7 TV network exclusively dedicated to management and leadership. Hsieh took over as CEO of Zappos in 1999, and the following year sales were $1.6 million. By 2009, only 10 years later, revenues reached $1 billion. The key to this extraordinary success, Hsieh insisted, was through consistent, careful, and systematic management of the culture of the company. In fact, Hsieh had a very particular business philosophy, which he summarized this way:

> *Culture is more important than strategy.*

For a person like me, who had lived his entire life thinking that strategy was not only the most important business variable, but almost the only one, that idea came as a real shock.

That same year, at another of our events, an innovation forum in New York, I interviewed the celebrated London Business School professor and director of the Management Innovation eXchange Gary Hamel. Although I'd known Gary since 2004, it was on that day in New York that I really started to understand the implications of his messages. In our conversation, he highlighted the need to reinvent management, and that the new ways to organize work had to foster and benefit from the passion, creativity, and commitment of employees. He insisted that management was actually a technology—a social one—that hadn't been upgraded in decades and that because needs had now changed significantly, particularly in regard to the role of human beings, it was therefore an economic and a moral imperative to reinvent management. One of the keys to this reinvention of management and leadership? To focus on the person.

In those years, in front of the crowd at various events, in formal private interviews, and in personal chats in hotel lobbies, planes, and homes, the more I spoke with business and political chiefs about what it takes to be a successful leader, the more I heard the same two things take center stage: culture and people.

Interestingly, however, despite this growing ubiquity of a stress on the importance of culture and people as crucial to successful business leadership, and even though culture and people had indeed become more of a focus with movements such as Conscious Capitalism and institutes like Great Place to Work, they were still not quite an overtly mainstream phenomenon. Few seemed to be writing about it then, and even fewer seemed to implement it in their business. It's really only been over the last few years that we've seen this idea enter the mainstream and heard leaders speaking, for instance, in the pages of the *Wall Street Journal* or the *Times'* business section, about the importance of culture and people.

In 2014 I wrote about this shift in the *Huffington Post*. In 2003, events focused on the frameworks of business strategy, marketing, and globalization. In 2014, the speeches and testimonies focused on organizations' people and the importance of caring for people in business. Though these ideas were not really new, for a long time they had not been generally accepted. At that 2014 event, however, they received a standing ovation. The message has finally become mainstream. In fact, a *Forbes* article from March 2015 traces the rise of the word *culture* over the last year as "one of the most important words in corporate board rooms," noting that "companies that focus on culture are becoming icons for job seekers" and therefore generating a new urgency for the business world to focus on culture.[6]

The call for business leadership to be less strategy-centered and more people- and culture-centered not only has become louder in recent years, but also has led us to understand how success has always been built on leadership that recognizes and mobilizes people and culture. That's why I offer you this book. As someone who has now been working on leadership with a focus on culture and people for nearly a decade, I want to share years' worth of information garnered from the greatest business and political leadership minds of our times, wisdom gathered from the anecdotes and reflections passed on to me in endless hours of conversation with the ultimate global political and business leaders, and spontaneous responses that embody the true guiding principles that have allowed leaders to change the world. I've extracted the most impactful concepts that have been shared with me and arranged them, accompanied by my own analysis, in a framework that helps bring the message home, setting off particular gems I've heard in *this bold italic font* so that you can find them easily, even if you're just flipping through.

But there's more! I want to add to this focus on people and culture an idea that I think is quite new and unique: One of the things I have realized is that leading through a focus on people and culture is actually all about *leading through emotion*. Although many leaders talk about generating passion or commitment, for instance, they usually do so in a "by the way" manner. For me, leadership that concerns people and culture is about generating certain emotions. So I want to share with you a novel idea that I will call *the new CEO*. The new CEO is the Chief Emotions Officer—because leadership is all about emotion, and culture is the overall environment in which one finds the aspects or elements on which one must concentrate to lead through emotion. That is, in order to be a successful leader in the twenty-first century, one must lead through emotion, which means fostering a strong culture. That is the lesson I have learned.

The world leaders I have interviewed throughout my career were all made of flesh and bone like you and me. Despite their power and success, these distinguished figures are emotional creatures; they also have fears, dreams, and fantasies. In my time with them, some shared personal stories, such as their dating exploits, and others revealed that they suffered from stage fright before giving an interview. Many more confessed that they weren't sure if anyone would be interested in what they had to say.

These "flaws" demonstrate that society's most prominent leaders are just common people—and that is great news for us all. In fact, I want to be clear that, throughout this book, when I refer to "the leader," I am actually talking about you and me. This role is not limited to any job post in particular. A leader is anyone who wishes to change reality, transform it, make it better. At the end of the day, it's not about trying to be like Jack Welch, Tony Hsieh, or any of the other renowned leaders you'll meet in this book. It's about realizing that we have the potential to keep growing and achieving more each day. It is about the desire for personal growth, to be a better person and to help others be better people as well. Ultimately, it is to build a better world with other people and for them. As corny as it sounds, that's leadership for me.

I hope that you will take this information and use it, in your own way, in the areas where you need it most so that it propels you to grow as a leader and as a person!

CHAPTER 1

CULTURE AND ITS RESULTS

Culture is not part of the strategy.
Culture is the strategy.
—Jim Collins, bestselling author
and leadership expert

CULTURE OR STRATEGY?
CULTURE *IS* THE STRATEGY

In this first section we will draw a distinction between *strategy* and *culture*—in other words, the "hard" variables and the so-called "soft" variables. We use the term *hard variables* for any elements that have to do with numbers and strategies, those variables that have to do with business design: how we'll compete, how we'll be financed, what the value proposition will be, how much we will spend on marketing, and how we'll allocate this spending. As for *soft variables*, they have to do with people, leadership, culture, emotion, values, and behavior. Strategy is the umbrella that unites all of the "hard" business variables, whereas culture does the same with the "soft" variables.

In this sense, strategy and culture are the two pillars of business success. Together, these two groups of variables determine how a business is run and ultimately its profitability. Relying on one alone would be like an athlete running an entire race jumping on one foot. Focusing simply on strategy, for instance, is akin to believing that you can win a horse race with a thoroughbred, even if you don't have a jockey, or that you're sure to win a boat race just because you have a great boat, even if you don't have a crew to sail it. Leaders should rely on both strategy and culture.

During a fascinating interview with Herb Kelleher, who is the cofounder and chairman emeritus of Southwest Airlines and who served as CEO of Southwest Airlines from 1971 to 2008, I asked him to explain the difference between strategy and corporate culture. We were seated in his spacious office, which looked more like a teenager's room than a CEO's: it was full of model planes, baseball paraphernalia, and abundant memorabilia. His response was a clear, simple story:

> *When Napoleon sat down in Paris with his generals around a table to decide how to invade Russia, they were making strategy. But what makes a million French troops march to Moscow? That is culture!*

Culture, then, is the driving force that can make a million men march to Moscow, full of pride, effort, dedication, and a desire for success, even when the odds are unknowingly stacked against them!

Yes, strategy and culture may be the two pillars of success for any company, but, as we discussed in the Prologue, an overwhelming majority of companies focus mainly on strategy and hard variables. Compared to the decades of emphasis put on strategy in the "business-as-usual" framework, culture has received significantly less attention among executives and business managers.

Certainly none of the hard variables or their corresponding frameworks include the human element in its full dimension. In fact, if we take a look at the different functional areas established by the "business-as-usual" school of thought, it seems as though *people* only appear from time to time, in sections such as "job description" or "performance evaluation." But the profound nature of *human* beings—their integrity, their emotions, their aspirations—are absent in those frameworks. Everything that has to do with managing people is put under a big umbrella called leadership. Instead of weaving people into each and every one of these variables, business-as-usual sets the human element aside as something to be dealt with separately.

A graphic representation of the situation might look something like Figure 1.1.

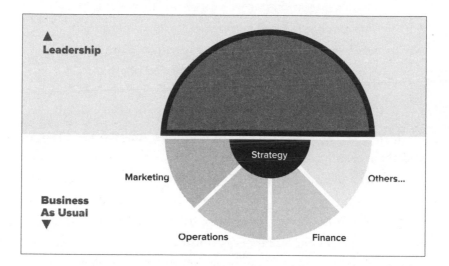

I am of course simplifying things. Culture and strategy are not wholly independent variables; they are intimately interrelated. Culture is an important variable in the strategy implementation process—it affects what people do, how they act, how they compete. *"Culture affects many things, true,"* explains Larry Hrebiniak, Emeritus Professor of Strategic Management at the Wharton School:

But it is also true that many things affect culture, and these things are also important for implementation. Strategy, industry and competitive forces, structure, incentives, controls, organizational talent and capabilities, etc. all interact and coalesce to affect strategy implementation and culture. Culture is both an independent, causal factor and a dependent

(continued)

> variable affected by other factors, variables, and forces. So, while focusing on culture is appropriate, it's also important to focus on other factors that are interdependent and important for implementation success. Successful strategy execution is the result of many interdependent factors and decisions.

However, companies have traditionally focused on strategy, and have therefore already extracted most of the potential value of strategic planning. Because most businesses have given an overwhelming importance to strategy and neglected culture, the opportunity is now there for culture to multiply results. If leaders become aware of the untapped resource of culture as well, they will unleash a supply of energy to help build and develop their business beyond its current reach.

In the final accounting, we are always left with the same question: What is the best way to create value—by leveraging culture or just focusing on strategy? When it comes to deciding which of these two groups has the highest potential to increase an organization's results, we have to ask ourselves: Which is more important, culture or strategy?

Well, you can already guess my answer, which is the same as one attributed to Peter Drucker: "Culture eats strategy for breakfast."

I insist that it is time for us all to focus on managing culture. Strategy is always overworked, so we get more out of focusing on culture. Its unused potential is why it's more important.

Former Hewlett-Packard CEO Carly Fiorina, who steered HP to become the world's largest manufacturer of personal computers during her tenure, emphasizes that soft variables are a crucial element of corporate success:

> *In the end, you have to pay attention*
> *to culture and behavior. I call this*
> *"the software of business."*

Considering Fiorina's concept of the *"software* of business," I've always wondered why there is such a focus on differentiating between "hard" and "soft" variables. Does that distinction allow us to better understand them? Where does the difference between the two lie? In the prologue for Cristiane Correa's book *Dream Big*, Jim Collins, the bestselling author and lecturer on leadership, gives an intriguing answer to the dilemma: "Culture is not part of the strategy. Culture is the strategy." Research and multiple examples show that when fully leveraged, strong cultures multiply results. In most cases, you need both the right strategy and a strong culture. However, if you recognize that culture can be a unique way of competing, you will discover that culture may in fact be the essence and heart of the strategy!

I would like to wrap this section up by giving you my answer to the question: Which is more important, culture or strategy? My answer—paraphrasing Bill Clinton—is "It's culture, stupid!" If you want to be the Chief Emotions Officer and lead through emotion, inspiring your team as Napoleon inspired his army, then fostering a strong culture is of primary import.

WHAT MAKES UP AN ORGANIZATION'S CULTURE?

We keep talking about culture. But what is culture? Even the most distinguished experts in the field, as well as the best practitioners of corporate culture, recognize how difficult it is to establish a comprehensive and generally accepted definition of corporate culture. Perhaps we should follow the guidance of Kelleher, who says:

> *Culture is hard to define, but perhaps a good way of thinking about it is to use the same definition that the United States Supreme Court once used for pornography: "You know it when you see it."*[1]

Indeed, what you actually see when you look at a business is not the culture, but its effects. Culture is like gravity. For most of us, it's hard to define—you can't see it, but you see and feel its effects all the time.

The difference between organizational culture and what we commonly refer to as culture is not only a matter of scale, but of scope, too. As a broader concept, culture functions on a societal scale as "the beliefs, customs, arts, etc., of a particular society, group, place, or time."[2] It reflects the "general values" and "behaviors" that are accepted and expected by a community—and, in many ways, acts as the backdrop for everything that occurs in a society. For example, culture defines everything from a given society's parameters regarding punctuality, the importance of one's time, and the way people dress to responsibility, expectations in terms of success, and even what is meant by the word *success*.

For Sir Ken Robinson, author, speaker, and international advisor on education, *"culture is the set of permissions that are given or not without having to ask for them."* This definition focuses on the rules that allow the behaviors, not only those that are accepted, but those that are expected as well. Although this is important, it can also be misleading. Anyone who believes that setting goals and objectives or correctly defining processes, tasks, and functions is enough to generate a positive culture is completely wrong. These must be coupled with a greater value or belief system. Therefore, culture could be generally defined as the common set of beliefs, thoughts, feelings, and emotions—all invisible—that result in a set of visible behaviors that give a group its identity.

Similarly, organizational culture would consist of a shared vision and set of beliefs and a set of common values and behaviors for all members of the organization. However, I prefer to define culture as the emotional impact you have on the people that belong to the organization.

A positive culture is anything that contributes to the development of a sense of purpose, a sense of belonging and community, an atmosphere of commitment and trust, self-esteem, pride, hope, passion, happiness, gratitude, and, in general, any other positive state of mind in your people.

You'll notice here that *culture generates emotions and states of mind.* Culture is the cause and effect that generates these positive emotions and states of mind in the members of an organization and therefore also a series of desirable behaviors. Culture is the realm where one manages people's hearts and minds.

If you're able to generate and manage such a culture, you'll take advantage of all your human capital. That's the power of culture! You've got to ignite the people! A positive culture will allow team members to discover and use their passion, creativity, and energy. When you're able to establish that *état d'esprit*, you maximize performance not only on an individual level, but also on a collective one. Individuals work better and teams are aligned and improve their performance. Through its particular values, culture wakes up people's strength and puts it to work toward the organization's vision. In the same vein as Herb's definition of pornography, where there is culture, you can see its effects!

Of course, there are numerous different kinds of cultures—from cultures based on service, people, or even a certain style to cultures based on performance and results, purpose, innovation, or ownership. The type of culture promoted at an organization will clearly have to do with its product, market, strategy, and even leadership personalities. For instance, an investment bank would not cultivate a culture of innovation, whereas it might be based around a culture of performance and results. We'll return to the different types of cultures in greater detail later when we discuss managing organizational culture. For now, though, I want to focus on how different types of cultures produce tangible results because, whether or not we can define culture or really paint an accurate picture of the emotions that make it up, we can certainly recognize its impact.

THE VALUE OF CULTURE: CULTURE MULTIPLES RESULTS

One reason that culture has not been as studied and spoken about in analyses of management and leadership as strategy may be because the soft variables of people and culture are arguably harder to measure than so-called hard variables. But if they are, in fact, harder to measure, what should we do? Ignore them? It is fascinating to see that because these intangible variables are indeed harder to grasp and measure, people tend to neglect them as though they were not key to the organization's performance.

The power of culture—the power of firing up people's hearts and souls, giving them a purpose and a sense of belonging—does not appear on any ledger sheets. Nonetheless, culture is a major asset. Though culture is a primary creator of value in a company, it is not always recognized as such because of the biases we have in measuring value creation. Indeed, in order to understand where the biggest opportunities to create value lie, we must first tackle how we measure that value creation.

We usually measure value creation in two ways. One is through the method of discounting future free cash flows. Most businesspeople would be aware of the impact of changes in costs or revenues on future cash flows, and in fact they are always reflected in the accounting statements.

The second way we can measure value creation in a business is by the accumulation of value in its assets. The difficulty here is that accounting standards try to be as conservative as possible, and, therefore, true asset valuations are hardly ever reflected in balance sheets. In the case of tangible assets such as a buildings or real estate, one is more likely to be aware of the evolution of their real value because they have an easier-to-estimate market value. Intangible assets are registered in the accounting books only when you pay for them.

Therefore, there are intangible assets that are not declared in the accounting books and for which we do not have an easy way to estimate market value. Three great examples of this are creating a renowned brand, consolidating a portfolio of loyal customers, and building a committed, loyal, and effective team of employees. The first two are customer-related assets; the latter is an asset related to culture. Despite the substantial value that all three represent, they go unnoticed by the accounting department,[3] which just looks at the balance sheet. This leads to a serious error in valuation. Moreover, it is also very likely that those assets will be undermanaged.

More, though, in some cases financial accounting may even lead us to the wrong conclusion or keep us from building value through culture. A real estate entrepreneur from Beverly Hills, Alan Long, founding partner of Dalton, Brown & Long Realtors—later DBL Realtors—shared a perfect example of this with me.

Originally from Chicago, Alan has degrees in chemistry and American literature from Loyola University. On vacations in Southern California, he met the owner of an established local real estate company who was so impressed by Alan's attitude, charisma, and salesmanship that he offered him an opportunity to sell real estate on Los Angeles's Westside. That caused a total career change. In 1987 Alan founded and built a successful real estate brokerage firm, achieving $3.3 billion in sales in 2003 with 600 brokers in nine offices around the Los Angeles area. In 2004, he received a purchase offer for his real estate agency, at which point he learned to value his company through the calculation of its Net Present Value. One day, he told me, "If I had done an MBA, I never would have been able to build and grow my company."

"What? Why do you say that?" I replied, surprised.

"Because a key contributor to my growth was giving my salespeople higher bonuses than the ones my competitors were offering when they closed a deal. It was a small additional percentage, but it really motivated them and allowed me to attract and retain the best people. When I learned how to value future cash flows, I realized that giving them that extra bit had 'cost' me several million dollars. I never would have done it!" he concluded. However, given the evidence of his effective management method, it was perfectly clear that it would have been a big mistake to eliminate those bonuses. At the end of the day, thanks in good part to a policy at odds with traditional business thinking and prevailing strategic values, he was able to build a great empire!

An entrepreneur in the South American real estate sector told me a similar story about the power of culture. We were talking about the importance of people, and he said: "Last month, I realized that one of my star salespeople had a long face. I went and asked him what was going on, and he told me that his daughter was having problems at school, which had him worried. 'Stay at home for a couple of months until you get it all figured out,' I said, and, of course, guaranteed him his salary." In his mind, the strategic alliance and the value of his best talents went far beyond one or two months' pay. This CEO was building and investing in the relationship between the company and its employees. But for most executives, everything in business is about transactions. It would be unthinkable to pay two months of salary without receiving anything in return!

Moral: The intangible assets that you create and develop— particularly a culture that values its people—do not appear in your accounting books. The accounting department is not effective at thoroughly measuring the creation of value and is therefore a very limited tool when planning how to create and manage a business. At the end of the day, it's obvious that any asset— whether it appears in the accounting books or not—ends up creating cash flow, whether it be through the business itself or by selling that asset. But you should always identify which factors generate value, particularly around culture, because its impact is often harder to identify even though a properly managed culture multiplies results.

The paradox comes when culture is measured and shown to have a tremendous impact on results, and when it becomes both a key way of "how a business is competing" and the very foundation of "how a business is unique." Yes, fostering a strong culture yields tangible economic results.

Why Is Culture So Important?

The message here is simple: *"Culture multiplies results."*

I would argue that this statement holds true whatever the objective, whether it is increasing sales, growing a company's net earnings, or enrolling more members in a nonprofit organization. The fact is, regardless of the goal you are working toward, a strong and positive culture has the power to multiply results.

By multiplying I don't mean a 10 or 15 percent increase. Attractive as those figures may seem, they don't even come close to the numbers I'm talking about. When I say multiply, I mean it in the most literal sense of the word because it's been proven that a properly managed corporate culture can exceed previously set targets by 100 or even 200 percent—that is, two to three times your original expectations! That's the magnitude of the impact we're talking about.

The Impact of Corporate Culture on Results

The following examples from my own experience in the business world, as well as the existing work in the field, should convince you of the remarkable impact of culture.

To begin with, I'd like to share a few studies that show the quantitative impact of culture. The first comes from the Great Place to Work Institute. Great Place to Work is a global human resources consulting, research, and training firm specializing in organizational trust. It was founded 25 years ago to identify the best companies in America to work for, based on the opinions of the companies' own employees.

Today, using a series of surveys, the Institute assesses the human resources practices of about 6,000 organizations with 10 million employees in 50 countries. It then analyzes this information and produces an annual ranking highlighting those work environments that have relationships based on trust, pride, and camaraderie—relationships identified as key drivers to improve an organization's business performance.

The Great Place to Work Institute defines the ideal workplace from the perspective of the leaders and from that of the employees because it has found that organizations around the world build great places to work by strengthening the relationship between leaders and employees, not by simply following a checklist of policies and practices.

From the perspective of how employees view the company, the most important criterion determining the ideal workplace is trust—employees should be able to trust the organization that they work for. That trust is created through management's credibility, the respect with which employees feel they are treated, and the extent to which employees expect to be treated fairly. The Institute maintains that a place that encourages trust also fosters feelings of pride and satisfaction for the work performed there.

How leaders perceive the organization is also crucial. According to the Institute, the ideal company to work for is one where the leader considers that the company's objectives are being achieved and that employees are giving their best, all within an atmosphere of camaraderie and trust.

According to the Institute's studies, investing in an organizational culture with an emphasis on trust yields tangible results. Not only do companies with the best working environments experience half as much voluntary turnover as the industry average (thus saving money on employee recruitment and training), but they also enjoy better financial results: some have reported more than double the return on investment, and in other cases, up to a 1,200 percent increase in annual profits.[4]

Given the impact of trust in establishing a strong business culture, the Institute recommends that companies *inspire, communicate with, and listen to* their employees in order to cultivate that trust. Additionally, leaders should *care for* their employees, helping them to *develop professionally and personally*, and then *thank them* for their services. In that way, managers and employees will be able to act as a group and as a family when it comes time to *hire, share, and celebrate*. I point these factors out here because, as we shall see later in the book, those recommended behaviors are actually the cornerstone of a great culture.

We see the impact of behaviors similar to these in the findings of the Rittenhouse Rankings Candor Survey. Inspired by Warren Buffet's focus on candor, Laura Rittenhouse measures the candor, honesty, and transparency in companies' communication, correlates those with financial performance, and ranks the companies. Over the past five years, top-quartile companies in the rankings have outperformed the S&P 500 by an average of 9.5 percent, suggesting that organizational cultures that breed behaviors like candor perform better.

In addition to these findings, other authors such as John Kotter and James Heskett[5] have proven that there is a positive correlation between culture and results. Kotter, a professor at the Harvard Business School and a renowned speaker on leadership, teamed up with HBS colleague Professor James Heskett to conduct an award-winning study on the relationship between culture and long-term economic growth. Reported in the groundbreaking book *Corporate Culture and Performance*, their findings offer compelling, quantitative proof that soft variables go far beyond creating a good working environment to underpinning outstanding economic growth.

As a part of Kotter and Heskett's study, 12 companies reported their results over a period of 11 years. Upon analyzing the numbers, Kotter and Heskett found that companies with a strong, well-managed corporate culture increased revenues by an average of 682 percent versus 166 percent for companies without a strong corporate culture. Likewise, the workforce in the first group grew by 282 percent, whereas the other group recorded only 36 percent growth. Even more, the two groups' cumulative stock prices reflected an overwhelming difference: those companies that fostered a corporate culture recorded an increase of 901 percent in their stock prices, while those that did not saw their stocks rise by only 74 percent. This is echoed by independent financial analysts, who claim that the publicly traded 100 Best Companies consistently outperform major stock indices by a factor of two.

Another interesting example of this tendency is Conscious Capitalism, the movement inspired by businesspeople like Whole Foods cofounder and CEO John Mackey, Harvard professor and former Medtronics CEO Bill George, Container Store CEO Kip Tindell, and Howard Schultz, chairman and CEO of Starbucks. Started almost 20 years ago, Conscious Capitalism upholds four primary principles: Higher Purpose, Conscious Leadership, Conscious Culture, and Stakeholder Orientation. Each of these elements is part of a unique culture centered on people and the well-being of all stakeholders, including the planet. Could you imagine a publicly traded company putting employees and the environment first two decades ago in the heyday of strategy-focused management? No way! But the financial results of conducting business in such a manner are impressive. In a study conducted by business professor Raj Sisodia, the 18 publicly traded companies out of the 28 consciously capitalist companies he identified outperformed the S&P 500 index by a factor of 10.5 over the years 1996 to 2011.[6] Tindell, CEO of The Container Store, which has an "employee first culture," lauds Conscious Capitalism's results: *"If you take the companies that are the most conscious capitalist in America and compare their performance with the S&P index over the last 15 years, they've outperformed it 14 times! Yes, this stuff works and doesn't just makes you feel good."*

According to Experts in the Field

Aside from the educational institutions and research centers that study corporate culture day in and day out, many entrepreneurs have publicly expressed the benefits of culture as an important way of boosting growth. This section offers you an overview of the examples and messages that leaders have shared in their interviews with me.

Jack Welch's Biggest Mistake: Not Considering the Culture

The first is actually a counterexample. I'm referring to the problems encountered by Jack Welch when he and General Electric decided to buy the Kidder, Peabody & Co. investment bank in 1986. The 120-year-old firm had seen no growth in its numbers for the last five years, while the industry had doubled. The deal was supposed to enable the financial firm to go after bigger business, especially on the corporate finance side. The addition of GE's massive capital resources and financial know-how would make Kidder "a whole new dynamic force in the securities industry,"[7] according to the experts.

But the reality proved to be harder than the rosy financial forecasts. Not long after GE acquired Kidder, the firm was implicated in an insider trading scandal. Although this was only one of the many insider trading scandals that characterized the time, Kidder's chief arbitrageur Richard Wigton had the dubious honor of being "the only executive handcuffed in his office as part of the trading scandal, an act that was later depicted in the movie *Wall Street*."[8] GE conducted an internal investigation, which resulted in the firing of Kidder chairman Ralph DeNunzio and two other senior executives. But that was not the end of the story. A few years later Kidder was again involved in a trading scandal related to the booking of false profits during the period 1990–1994. Following the rush of bad press coverage, GE decided to sell Kidder's assets to PaineWebber, and GE received a net of $90 million for a firm that it had purchased for $600 million.

Jack characterizes the debacle of the Kidder acquisition as the "biggest failure" of his professional career. That's saying something, considering that during Welch's time at the helm of GE, he made 600 acquisitions.[9] In a conversation at his Boston home in late 2005, Jack confided to me:

> I made acquisitions that didn't work, and I learned from it. Sometimes I bought a company that had a bad culture and that was the failure. When we bought Kidder, Peabody and Co., I was looking at the numbers and not at the culture. Investment banking was very different; they had a culture of bonuses.

He had ignored the culture in favor of the numbers and readily admitted that it had come back to haunt him.

If you think about all that Welch has achieved throughout his career, this episode makes very clear how important culture has to be in order for it be the cause of the greatest failure of "the most admired CEO of all times." Was culture really responsible for undermining all of the quantitative analyses performed by Welch and his group of advisors when they were considering such a substantial purchase? Is culture so powerful that it can cause the masters of business management to fail? And if culture is so important, again, why isn't it taken enough into account in various models of strategy?

Jack Welch's Key to Success: A Culture of Winning

We have seen that Welch attributed his business problems to his failure to consider culture, but what about his success at GE? During his 20 years as the head of GE, he transformed the company, taking its market value from $14 billion to over $400 billion, making it the greatest value creation in corporate America's history. What is the key that led Jack to transform General Electric into a winning company?

Let's see if GE's business strategy was behind its success. Welch defined his business strategy as aiming to be "number one or number two in any given sector," but according to many business management experts, this doesn't even meet the minimum requirements of a strategy. Think back to our previous definition of strategy. It's hard to reconcile with Jack's "strategy." "Being number one or number two in every business it operates in" ultimately doesn't answer the question of "how is it going to compete" or in what ways it is unique. Moreover, there was never a single global strategy for GE as a group. That would have been impossible. If you have several hundred businesses that range from lightbulbs to jet engines, each one of those businesses has a strategy—that is, a specific way of competing—that is most certainly different from one business to the other. How could GE have had the same strategic advantage in each of its hundreds of businesses?

But if being number one or number two is not really a strategy, then what is it? It is culture. It is an expression of a larger culture at GE. This culture is the "Culture of Winning." Yes, the real difference that set GE apart from other companies was its common culture of winning. Everybody likes to win, so the culture of winning is very powerful. The constant pursuit of victory allows teams to see success as something tangible, thus enhancing their results. And Jack certainly got results, exponential results.

This culture emanated from Jack's personality, personal philosophy, and vision. He explains:

> *Well, I have a philosophy built on four pillars. First, you define the mission you are working toward. Then you put together a set of behaviors you'll require from your employees. Therefore, your mission and your values define where you are going to go and how you are going to get there, the how and the why. Then I have something that I call candor. Candor is where you stop all the nonsense, and you tell everybody straight-on what you are thinking and what you are doing. . . . Then comes differentiation, both hard and soft. For the hard, you differentiate your businesses and your products, making hard calls on where you put your money. . . . With candor comes differentiation with people, where you take care of your best to an extreme. . . . You train the 70 percent in the middle, showing them the way to the top, and to the bottom 10 percent, you counsel people out. You can't have differentiation without candor.*

At GE, Jack set up a system to put this philosophy into action: a culture of winning based on a set of strong values and behaviors, including candor and differentiation, to achieve performance. All of these elements were important in building GE's particular overall culture.

What all companies belonging to the GE Group had in common was that they were the leader or number two in their businesses. If they were not, the Group had to fix them, sell them, or close them. Simple as that. The goal of having companies in the portfolio that were number one or two in their markets was to create and then bolster the culture of winning.

As author and lecturer Bill Conaty, senior vice president of human resources at GE for nearly 15 years, explains, *"Another aspect of the culture Jack Welch propelled was 'Here we are winners; losers have to go' and establishing a system of measuring performance that was the 20/70/10. I think differentiation is key for a culture driven by performance."*

Jack promoted a focus on talent growth, recruiting and keeping the best people. To ensure that, he put in place a performance evaluation system called 20/70/10. Every year, the company ranked employees in terms of performance and behaviors. The company gave to the top 20 percent all of the rewards: promotions, wage increases, perks, and bonuses, among others. To the middle 70 percent, the company gave recognition for their work and encouraged them to continuously improve their performance. Finally, the bottom 10 percent were requested to look for a job elsewhere. Thus, year after year, he strengthened the talent pool within each of his businesses.

Jack's firing up people's hearts and souls, getting them behind a vision, and putting in place the necessary elements to win across every one of GE's businesses was what created one of the most successful corporate cultures ever and was ultimately the origin and cause behind that history-making value creation.

Herb Kelleher: The Culture of People

Another very interesting case through which to evaluate the tremendous impact of culture on performance is Herb Kelleher's Southwest Airlines. Who among you would like to acquire a company in a sector that has faced decades of serious profitability problems, as well as the bankruptcy of leading competitors? My first reaction would be, "Not even if they gave it to me for free!" But what a terrible mistake that would be if the company were Southwest.

According to *Money* magazine, out of all the companies featured on the S&P 500 Index between 1972 and 2002, Southwest Airlines enjoyed the highest return to shareholders.[10] For instance, $10,000 invested in Southwest in 1972 was worth $10,200,000 in 2002, an average increase of 25.99 percent per year! I think we would all agree that's a pretty good return on investment! And if you consider that Southwest had the best return to shareholders not only in the floundering airline industry, but among the biggest 500 companies in America, then you really can grasp the scope of Southwest's achievement.

Was it the strategy that made it so successful and profitable?

Kelleher, cofounder and former Southwest Airlines CEO, attributes only part of his company's success to a 10-word strategy: Southwest is a "low-fare, high-frequency, short-haul, point-to-point carrier." The airline kept the same strategy for over 40 years. As such, it is hard to differentiate and ends up being, from a purely strategic perspective, a commodity type, and it is hard to make healthy margins in a commodity business. We, then, have to look for the cause of such profitability elsewhere.

During an interview at his office in Dallas, I heard Herb's amazing story of success and had the opportunity to ask him what, in his eyes, was the source of Southwest's competitive advantage. He explained:

> *I always thought that our esprit de corps, the attitude of our employees, was one of our biggest competitive advantages. You know, people like to be treated nice; they like to be treated well, and our people do that from the goodness of their hearts. And that is our advantage over other carriers.*

I was fascinated by his conviction and the pride with which he referred to his company and people. It was a mixture of joy and fun, the pride of having built something much bigger than himself—a culture based on people that has led to enormous success. He was relaxed, very comfortable, always with a smile on his face. As he would say a couple of months later during the tango lessons I gave him in New York, *"My passion is people!"* And it's your people who make up your culture.

I share Herb's belief that the root of Southwest's competitive advantage is its culture. Indeed, Southwest's "industry days" offer compelling proof of this. Kelleher told me that "industry days" were special days when the company opened its doors and shared its processes and operational practices with managers from other organizations—*including its competitors*. At first glance, it doesn't make sense for a company to share its processes, but even when Southwest revealed its secrets, no competitor was able to replicate them. In Herb's opinion, there was nothing to be afraid of:

> *Given enough time and money, your competitors can duplicate almost everything you've got working for you. They can hire away some of your best people. They can reverse-engineer your processes. But the only thing they cannot duplicate is your culture. They can copy what we do, but not who we are or what we believe in, and without that it's not enough.*

What was unique about Southwest was not its processes, but its culture, the airline's unique way of having people as the cornerstone of the company. This is what cannot be replicated.

That is why, even if we go beyond the examples offered by Jack Welch at General Electric or the different situations that Herb Kelleher faced at Southwest Airlines, any company will pride itself on having a strong culture that gives it a competitive advantage.

From a Culture of Sheer Talent to a Culture of People and Values

But don't take my word for it. Listen to Tony Hsieh, CEO of Zappos.com, the successful online shoe retailer, on his current success and past struggles. For Hsieh, culture is more important than strategy, and a participatory culture centered on people and values is preferable to one just centered on professional excellence and hierarchy. He once told me in a very casual but extremely informative televised interview we did from a hotel in New York:

> *Since the beginning at Zappos.com the culture has always been the most important thing, and to this day it's the company's number one priority. Our belief is that if we get the right culture, most of the other things, like delivering a great service or constructing a long-lasting brand, will be a natural consequence. Obviously it depends on which is your culture is.*

Hsieh should know. He now makes culture his priority, but it wasn't always that way for him. In fact, one might say that, like Jack Welch, he learned the hard way.

In 1996 Tony founded an Internet advertising network called LinkExchange with fellow Harvard graduate Sanjay Madan. LinkExchange grew very quickly. Within 90 days it had over 20,000 participating web pages, and by 1998 the site had over

400,000 members. Initially Tony enjoyed working at LinkExchange because he would hire his friends or friends of friends. When he ran out of that talent pool, his belief was that the best way to achieve continuous growth was, in his words, to "hire the best." So that's exactly what he did: hire a great number of talented engineers and professionals to work in his organization—the best he could find at the top of the field.

However, Tony soon realized that LinkExchange's workplace environment wasn't what he wanted. In fact, he felt unhappy at his own company. In particular, he felt uncomfortable with the people he had hired. The majority of the headcount had been hired because they were the "best in the field," but with that had come big egos that wanted nothing more than results and money, come what may. These were different values from the ones by which Tony wished to live. He realized that he wanted to work with people who had sheer talent and excellent professionalism, but great human values, as well. He wanted to work in a company whose culture was friendly and family-like. He realized that he had created a talent-driven, authoritative, and cutthroat company when what he really wanted was one driven by passion, people, and vision.

Here I think it is important to note that the culture Hsieh desired reflected his personal values. That is, the traits Hsieh was looking for in the team members who would make up his company were both a reflection of his own values and, I would argue, the characteristics that made Hsieh a successful leader in the first place. In fact, most great leaders look for the same traits and values they have in their employees; such complementarity is crucial to the creation of a strong and winning culture.

Although Hsieh had founded LinkExchange and was the CEO, he realized it would be very difficult to change the culture, as a significant culture change would have necessitated a significant change in the teams—a serious shakeup of the company.

Discontented with this situation, Tony woke up one day and realized that he didn't want to work at LinkExchange any longer. Soon thereafter, he sold his shares to Microsoft in a transaction valued at $265 million and left the company.

Two years later, Hsieh invested in and became the CEO of a small online shoe retailer that clocked sales of $1.6 million for the year 2000. This was Zappos.com. Having learned the importance of culture, he now had the opportunity to focus on building teams with people he liked working with. Hsieh told me:

> *Our priority is culture over strategy. We hire or fire based on our central values, independently from job performance and even if the employee is a star.*

With this guiding philosophy, he grew Zappos to an extremely successful company. Nearly 10 years after Tony joined, Zappos had reached $1 billion in sales and, in July 2009, he sold the company to Amazon.com in a deal valued at approximately $1.2 billion.

The reason behind this tremendous success was Zappos's culture, with its focus on people—and not strategy. We will return to Zappos and take a closer look at the unique elements that constitute its culture in Chapter 7, but, for now, let's sum up the moral of this unique story.

Moral: The best culture is not the one that promotes excellence simply by hiring the best professionals. The best culture creates an environment of collaboration, open and honest relationships among employees, and respect for certain human values. The best employees are not necessarily those that stand out purely for their technical skills. The best are those capable of doing the job, adhering to the company's values, and living according to its corporate culture on a daily basis.

Seeing Is Believing: Where Corporate Culture Determines Results

Despite decades of focus on strategy as the determinant of results, culture as the chief tool for business success is perhaps more common than anyone would ever have thought. Beyond Jack, Herb, and Tony, many other great leaders make this point.

Take Lou Gerstner, for instance. As chairman and CEO of IBM from 1993 to 2002, Gerstner turned the information technology giant around by leveraging all of IBM's businesses capabilities—hardware, software, and services—to deliver integrated technology solutions. During that period IBM's market capitalization rose from $29 billion to $168 billion. Gerstner came from a strategy consulting background, and when he took office he was of the opinion that culture was one among "several important elements in any organization's makeup and success—along with vision, strategy, marketing, financials, and the like." But he learned during his time at IBM that corporate culture "is not part of the game: It is the game. In the end, an organization is nothing more than the collective capacity of its people to create value."[11]

Carlos Brito, CEO of Anheuser-Busch InBev, who grew his company to become the global leader in the beer sector, with a quarter of the world market share, acknowledges that culture is the factor that differentiates failure or stability from true success. He says:

[T]he only thing that can explain differences in performance is what we call the dream-people-culture.

Although all the examples I've mentioned are great illustrations of the impact that culture has on organizations, I'd like to talk about a very special case: The Virgin Group.

Virgin: A Group Built Around Its Culture

The Virgin Group is a particularly interesting case in which an intrepid entrepreneur created a massive (and massively profitable) group of over 400 extremely different businesses that range from music and vodka to space tourism and financial services. Founder and CEO Richard Branson started his immensely successful group as a mail-order record company and ultimately founded the rebellious and cool music label Virgin Records in 1973. From there he jumped industries and entered the risky sky of airline carriers, founding Virgin Atlantic Airways, which he boldly followed in 2004 by founding Virgin Galactic, a company devoted to space travel; equally ambitiously, Branson purchased his first hotel in 2011, inaugurating Virgin Hotels.

In a conversation backstage at Radio City Music Hall, just before we went on, he said to me: "Our diversification strategy was really a *vertical disintegration*, because our new businesses have nothing to do with our old ones." Indeed, there is no strategic link between a record label launching an airline, then a phone company, and finally, Virgin Active, an international chain of health clubs. So, if the reasons behind each new company cannot be understood from a strategic perspective, a different point of view is required to really grasp the key to their diversification.

As in the case of Jack Welch's GE, with its diverse set of businesses across the globe and only the common culture of "winning" to unify it, The Virgin Group's glue is also its culture. Its culture became the driving force of its growth strategy! But unlike GE, Virgin's culture is based on its founder's attributes: competitive, fun, rebellious, and cool.

Virgin's core values are innovation, value for money, quality, fun, and adventure, which totally mirror the founder's style. For instance, Branson loved listening to music and believed that people traveling in an airplane shouldn't be bored, so Virgin worked to make flights more amusing. Entertainment was, indeed, an important element of Virgin Atlantic's success during the 1980s and early 1990s. Beyond the availability of music, passengers were entertained with videos and, in some cases, live performances from mimes or musicians. Recently, the cast of the American television series *Fly Girls* served cocktails on a flight en route to Las Vegas, while passengers got a sneak peek of the show's first episode. But these kinds of entertainments pale in comparison with some of Virgin's other fun offerings. For the inaugural Virgin Atlantic flight, for instance, Branson dressed up as a pilot and convinced passengers he was flying the plane. On another occasion, he dressed up as a flight attendant, replete with short skirt and hyper-red lipstick.

Virgin Group's strength comes from trying to help people have the best time they can where they least expect it and from facing challenges in whatever industry they are competing in. This perhaps explains the impetus behind developing Virgin Galactic, the world's first commercial space line.

Moreover, as Virgin continued to grow, Branson and his initial partners discovered that working in something that was cool and that they were passionate about could have the added benefit of creating a culture that provided customers with great service. Branson surrounded himself with great people who shared his vision and his passion, people committed to collaborate with others to bring his dreams to life—and to have fun while doing it. Because happy and healthy people perform better, identify with what they represent, and tend to tell others about and share this happiness, the Virgin culture became infectious. It was cool to be a Virgin employee, and it was cool to be one of its customers.

This creates value and increases success, recognition, and sales. The Virgin Group went from a single nonprofit business in 1967 to a £100 million revenue record label in 1973. In the 1980s the group was made up of 100 companies, and by 1993 The Virgin Group achieved £1 billion in revenues. Entering the new millennium, 24,000 employees took the company to a £3 billion revenue mark. Today, the 50,000 employees that make up Virgin's more than 400 companies produce revenue of over £15 billion. How's that for confirmation that culture multiplies results?

We clearly see in this example something we'll explore in more detail later: that culture is at the heart of the brand—or the other way around: the brand is the expression of the culture. Furthermore, both culture and brand become the essence of Virgin's strategy—its unique way of competing in the market.

Virgin seems to be the embodiment of the idea Jim Collins repeated in the Radio City Music Hall:

> **Culture is not part of the strategy. Culture is the strategy.**

Strategy used to be considered the paramount favorite for business success. But, throughout the chapter, we have reviewed why culture, a so-called soft variable and up to now generally neglected by the business world, multiplies results. Culture, which is the purpose, emotions, values, and behaviors that fire up people's hearts, ends up being such a determining force of performance that the best way to express this importance is with the aid of the hard variables: once again, culture is the strategy!

CHAPTER 2

LEADERSHIP THROUGH EMOTION: THE NEW CEO

A team is a state of mind, a mood. And an individual is fundamentally a state of mind too.
—**Jorge Valdano,** member of the Argentine championship soccer team at the 1986 World Cup in Mexico and former general manager at the Real Madrid

I'm confident that you've found the examples of the fundamental way in which culture multiplies results interesting, but I suspect that you're also asking yourself, "OK, but how? How does culture multiply results?" Through leadership! Leadership multiplies results. Yes, we've always known that, but we've always been led to think of leadership accomplishing results predominantly through strategy. I want to offer what I believe is a novel answer to the question.

As we saw in the last chapter, culture generates emotions, so, inasmuch as your role as a leader is to create and manage your company's culture, your role as a leader is essentially *to produce certain emotions*. Leaders multiply results by creating cultures because cultures generate emotions, such as a sense of purpose, pride, and trust. These emotions align people behind a common vision and series of values and behaviors and give them the energy, determination, and proper states of mind to act. Think of it this way: as a leader at any level, your overarching responsibility is to shape emotions; these emotions undergird and guide the organizational culture, which in turn generates the desired results. That is, cultures both are created by and create emotions, and it's these cultures that have a tremendous impact on the success or failure of a company's endeavors. Understanding emotions and how they play a consequential role in people's behaviors is therefore very important.

WHAT ARE EMOTIONS?

Reflecting on Southwest's "industry days," when the competition came to study his company's processes and organization, Herb Kelleher said:

> *Most of them were looking for a formula that you could put on a blackboard. But it has to proceed from the heart, not the head.*

If emotions are such a crucial part of creating a successful culture, then we should probably ask what emotion is. A survey of popular dictionaries reveals a focus on emotion as the subjective experience of a forceful feeling accompanied by physiological and behavioral changes.[1] Because of the role played in emotion by biochemicals such as dopamine, oxytocin, endorphins, or noradrenaline,[2] it is often associated with and considered influential on mood, temperament, and personality, and, perhaps most crucially for a manager, it is frequently "the driving force behind motivation, positive or negative."[3]

This idea of emotion as a driving force stems from its etymology. *Emotion* comes from the Latin *emotĭo* or "the state of being moved out of rest or put in motion." Emotions, then, are the physical and mental reactions that lead human beings to move, to act. In this book I will follow this sense, employing the word *emotions* as akin to driving factors, the psychophysical states of mind that drive performance. I will focus on how emotion drives people, or more particularly, how it impacts performance.

Obviously, there are positive and negative emotions—from trust, pride, belonging, purpose, passion, and confidence, on the one hand, to distrust, dissatisfaction, disengagement, helplessness, frustration, anxiety, and apathy, on the other. Emotions consequently impact a team's performance in both positive and negative ways.

EMOTIONS HAVE AN IMPACT ON PERFORMANCE

Sports present an interesting venue through which to see the impact of emotion on performance. Jorge Valdano, who became coach and general manager of the Real Madrid club and a leadership guru after being a member of the Argentine championship soccer team at the 1986 World Cup in Mexico, clearly expresses the impact that emotions have on performance:

> *A team is a state of mind, a mood. And an individual is fundamentally a state of mind too. In football you often see players that have the trust of their coach, the respect of the journalists, the love of their fans, and they achieve excellence. They change teams and they lose those external supports and they can just be mediocre. And we are talking of individuals. When we speak of many individuals, the impact of their state of mind can appear to be even miraculous. It is amazing what a state of mind can achieve, both positively and negatively, in the results of a team.*

He sums up:

> *When people feel what they do, when people feel committed, from that attitude they are able to inspire the rest of the group.*

In sports, it is easy to see how positive and negative emotions can have a significant impact on a team's results. Thanks to emotions, athletes are able to form a cohesive group with a common goal—or they don't and they lose. Plus, emotions are fundamental in the sports world because they release endorphins, dopamine, and other hormones that inhibit pain to increase muscular performance and achieve victory.

But maybe this example makes you wonder: Why do I need to release endorphins and "increase muscular performance" when what I really want is to increase my performance as a marketing analyst? Why do I need emotion in the office? Isn't this type of job 100 percent intellectual and rational? Does that mean that emotions are irrelevant in certain disciplines?

Human beings usually go through a rational thinking process before they make a decision, which then results in a behavior. Or so we were taught to believe. What actually happens is that our body's chemistry is constantly interfering with that pure rational thinking and decision-making process. External and internal factors—be they physical threats in the environment or complex internal states of mind—alter the levels of hormones, neurotransmitters, and other biochemicals, modifying or influencing the decisions we make and our consequent behaviors.

The effects of these changes in biochemicals on our being are what we call emotions. The hormones and neurotransmitters that are triggered under certain conditions correspond to a given emotion and predispose the body for certain behaviors. That is, circumstances trigger the biochemicals that are "felt" as what we call an emotion, and that predisposes our body for a given action. Whether the actions resulting from the emotions are positive or negative will depend on factors of which a good leader must be aware.

Let's consider two examples. First, take the hormone and neurotransmitter adrenaline—a substance that we secrete when we feel challenged, afraid, surprised, angry, or anxious. Adrenaline can have a positive or negative effect on function depending on the emotional circumstances dictating its levels. Consider a bear attack. In preparing the body for fight or flight, the amygdala orders the adrenal gland to secrete high levels of adrenaline, which accelerates the heart rate in order to take the blood rapidly to the arms and legs. At the same time, the adrenaline also causes the limbic system to switch off the neocortex and its cognitive functions. We don't think; we just fight or run. This is the survival instinct of primitive man over rational man. But though elevated levels of adrenaline may be just the thing you need when faced with a hungry bear, it's not so clear that the results will be as helpful or positive when confronted with a brashly competitive or uncivil coworker.

The productive impact of cortisol is equally circumstantial and dependent upon its level. Although its main action is related to metabolic and cardiovascular activity, it is better known—together with adrenaline—as the main hormone produced under stressful conditions. This can be both positive and negative. For instance, cortisol plays a role, along with adrenaline, in "fight-or-flight" situations such as a robbery, an accident, or, yes, a bear attack. In these scenarios, it is positively critical for survival. Fortunately, most of these sorts of stress situations are relatively infrequent and transitory. Indeed, the boost of cortisol associated with short-term stress situations can be helpful. "Good stress" during short-term periods is usually associated with situations where the individual is attempting to accomplish something. Under these circumstances, it appears to be associated with improved cognitive performance, sharpening the brain's alertness. "Some amounts of stress are good to push you just to the level of optimal alertness, behavioral and cognitive performance," says Daniela Kaufer, associate professor of integrative biology at UC Berkeley.[4] However, "bad stress" or chronic stress is generally thought to be noxious and a risk factor for a variety of mood and anxiety disorders. The levels of cortisol and adrenaline associated with it narrow down our focus, impede our concentration, and cause our cognitive abilities to deteriorate. Prolonged bad stress affects memory and induces changes in the brain that can not only hinder performance significantly but also actually contribute to serious illness.

Indeed, negative emotions literally make humans dumber because they chemically intercept our ability to use logic, and that anxiety blocks creativity and reasoning. As Charles S. Jacobs, author of *Management Rewired*, notes:

> *The brain operates very differently when we are down than when we are happy: it slows down, our vision narrows, we don't see the big picture anymore.*

When people feel afraid, anxious, or unhappy, they make silly mistakes because their brains aren't working like they usually do. Fear puts us on guard and makes us mistrust others. In the face of an external environment that triggers negative emotions, our brains struggle to perform at even normal levels. As researcher Christine Porath notes, "[P]eople working in an environment characterized by incivility miss information that is right in front of them. They are no longer able to process it as well or as efficiently as they would otherwise."[5]

Positive emotions can do the exact opposite, so it is important to understand the role played by hormones like endorphins, dopamine, serotonin, and oxytocin in promoting emotions such as trust, joy, pride, commitment, and happiness. Physical exercise, for instance, triggers endorphins, which block physical pain and help us keep pushing ourselves to where we need to be. If you've ever had a "runner's high," you know this feeling. When we accomplish a goal, our body triggers dopamine. Every time we see a finish line or milestone, cross something off our to-do list, or see movement toward our goals, we get that shot of dopamine! We call those emotions pride, commitment, and satisfaction. When we experience personal and social achievements, such as public acknowledgment in front of friends and family, we get a shot of serotonin. We call those emotions pride and joy. Moreover, creating those very bonds, building trust, and reinforcing friendships are associated with high levels of oxytocin. In the end, when people feel positive emotions, they perform better on cognitively demanding tasks; plus, they are more likely to consider the community than to just consider themselves.

It's not hard to see here the radically different and often forceful impacts produced by the emotions. Emotions are the "blood" of any organization. Just as a blood disorder can harm or even cripple a body, "bad blood" can cripple an organization. As Herb says, ***"Bad attitudes metastasize throughout the organization no matter where they are located. We choose attitude over all other attributes."*** Therefore, it is the duty of a leader to understand that she can control and use certain stimuli to create the appropriate emotions that, in turn, increase performance at work.

Reflecting on the magnitude of the impact of emotion, I realized that I was ignoring the evidence: How many times had I seen companies where trust had been broken, causing employees to take a defensive attitude and do only what was necessary rather than taking risks or dreaming? How many times had I seen professionals working under an enormous amount of pressure in directionless teams or hostile environments make silly mistakes or drastically underperform?

Throughout my business career, I have witnessed a number of situations such as these. For example, I once saw a marketing analyst with an excellent academic background and very good professional experience who made silly mistakes. He responded defensively when he received feedback and was suspicious of the team. In short, he was very hard to work with. Why? Because he was constantly under tremendous pressure, afraid of losing his job, and had to confront an abusive boss on a daily basis.

Six months later, that same marketing analyst was the star because his professional qualities had finally come to light. Working under a boss who oriented and supported him and surrounded by a trustworthy group of coworkers, this same professional began performing with great effectiveness. The difference, of course, was his emotional state; it was the contrast between his previous experience with a boss who mistreated him and the support he found in his new working environment. This shows the tremendous power and impact of a leader who can change individual and group performance by creating the appropriate states of mind and emotions in each of the team members. That's why managing both positive and negative emotions is an essential part of team culture and a crucial aspect of any professional performance. Even if we are not aware of it, appropriate leadership actions reduce the excess of "bad" neurotransmitters like cortisol and adrenaline and foster good ones like serotonin and oxytocin. And poor leadership actions do the opposite, pushing up cortisol for extended periods of time and, as with our market analyst, drastically reducing performance.

THE NEW CEO: CHIEF EMOTIONS OFFICER

This is why, as a leader, our job is to manage emotion. That's right. Leaders should manage both their own emotions and their team members' emotions. Leaders have to be aware of the impact that their projects, actions, and decisions have on their team members' emotions and states of mind. They must use that awareness as a starting point for managing those emotions—and for provoking emotions in others. In fact, the biggest challenge for all of us is to be aware of and properly manage the impact of both our own emotions and those felt or expressed by others in the workplace.

Leaders are responsible for creating an environment and work practices that encourage positive states of mind. People will naturally look for situations where they experience positive emotions, so a leader should aim to promote all of the positive emotions, contain or transform the negative ones into actions that move the organization toward better results, and contribute to the personal growth of all the organization's members. A leader must understand these positive states of mind, as well as the emotions that underlie them, and promote a culture that leverages these motivating factors, improving individual and collective performance.

Until a few years ago, most people would have said that the real challenge concerning emotions in the workplace was to hide them or get rid of them. But nowadays, I think there is more awareness that human beings cannot just shut off a piece of themselves when they go to the office, and that workers will only be able to reach their fullest human potential when they use their emotions. That's why psychologist and author Dan Goleman insists, *"Emotional intelligence is key for leadership."*

Indeed, whether we're talking about being empathetic and being sensitive toward people or knowing how to listen and genuinely care for people, we are really talking about emotions, emotional connections, and emotional relations. I firmly believe there is great potential for a leader to develop his or her leadership skills by taking advantage of this "emotional toolbox." The best leaders do in fact take complete advantage of the full range of emotional tools available. Without a doubt, Jack Welch and Herb Kelleher are experts in using their own and their teams' emotions to manage and create cultures.

Echoing something he had asserted in one of our interviews, Goleman explained at a keynote address: "In setting the stars apart from the average, emotional intelligence is twice as important as the cognitive abilities." The introduction to Goleman's bullet list for the *New York Times* on "How to Be Emotionally Intelligent" sums up his idea in the following way: "What makes a great leader? Knowledge, smarts and vision, to be sure. To that, Daniel Goleman, author of *Leadership: The Power of Emotional Intelligence*, would add the ability to identify and monitor emotions—your own and others'—and to manage relationships. Qualities associated with such 'emotional intelligence' distinguish the best leaders in the corporate world, according to Mr. Goleman."[6]

Emotional management is central to a strong culture. Indeed, emotional management is the greater key. It plays a role in any aspect of management. Consequently, I would say that every leader should be a "CEO" in the sense of "Chief Emotions Officer." In order to lead his organization to reach its full potential, the Chief Emotions Officer should be the emotional leader, managing the working environment—the culture and its emotions—just as much as, if not more than, managing processes and functions!

In my years of leadership, I have come to understand that the primary emotions one wants to create and instill are a sense of purpose, a sense of belonging and gratitude, commitment and trust, self-esteem, and pride and engagement. These are five emotional states that a leader has to be particularly attentive to if she wants a high-performing organization, and indeed they correspond to what we will see are the five key roles of the Chief Emotions Officer.

In order to effectively picture the Chief Emotions Officer, you will need to ask yourself the following questions, as the answers provide a sketch of the emotional mandates she has:

- How can you give people a *sense of purpose*? Create a dream, a reason. Give them an important direction within the organization. This gives them pride and hope in their mission.

- How can you give them a *sense of belonging and gratitude*? Create a community with an identity and common values. Take care of each person's well-being.

- How can you achieve *commitment* and *trust*? Relentlessly communicate who you are and what you are aiming for. Listen to your people and be empathetic. Have clear values and practice what you preach. Truly connect with your team members; be frank and honest. Walk your talk.

- How can you improve *self-esteem*? Establish practices that favor delegation and learning, and a support system for when errors are made. Recognize each person for what he or she brings to the table.

- How can you develop *pride* and *engagement*? Develop a culture unique to your organization that fosters pride in belonging to it and that creates commitment in every person on your team.

In other words, an organization with a culture of high performance is one where people find meaning in their work, trust their coworkers, and enjoy that community and feel proud to belong to it.

But how do you create this? Well, in my years of listening to world leaders, I began to identify ideas and roles that came back over and over again.

THE ORIGINS OF MY NEW LEADERSHIP MODEL

We have seen how the business-as-usual model does not account for people, their emotions, or the overarching importance of culture. We also saw the impact leaders have on people by creating different emotions and states of mind that allow individuals and teams to perform significantly better. We also discussed how business-as-usual has historically tossed anything having to do with the nature of human beings and managing it into a big catch-all bucket known as "leadership" and left it there to stagnate.

Now, I'd like to propose a new framework to replace that big, ambiguous bucket with a series of well-defined roles that will be much more effective in helping the Chief Emotions Officer manage the people who work in his organization.

The framework I will propose comes as the result of thousands of hours of conversations with the great leaders I've had the privilege to know and work with, as well as the first-rate companies I've been able to study. In order for you to get a sense of how I arrived at the five key tasks or roles of the effective leader that will serve as the heart of this book, I want to let you eavesdrop on four of the most exemplary conversations that I've cherry-picked for you. In them, you'll hear what some of the most celebrated and effective leaders of the last 30 years feel are the roles most critical to a leader's success.

Leadership in the Words of the Leaders

In an onstage conversation at Radio City Music Hall in 2008, Tony Blair, prime minister of the United Kingdom from 1997 to 2007, explained to me:

As a leader, what you owe the people you are leading—
what you owe them in the ultimate analysis—is the truth
as you see it and the right decision as you perceive it.

During an interview in a hotel bar after an event in Mexico City in 2010, former secretary of state Colin Powell told me that everything he knew about leadership he had learned during his first months at the military academy at Fort Benning:

They drilled into us that leadership is all about the
followers and that the main role of the leader is to
serve them; the followers get the job done, achieve
the goals, and, at the end of the day, are ultimately
responsible for the success of the organization.

He also explained that followers *"want to know what the mission is, what do you want them to achieve, what is the purpose of our operation."*

Jack Welch offers his own reflection on these leadership roles. In an interview in his apartment overlooking Central Park, he told me:

You have to know that when you are a leader, it's not
about you. It's about them, your people—always caring
about how they are developing, how they are growing,
how they are building. You've got to be encouraging
idea flow; you've got to get your team on board with a

(continued)

61

> *philosophy that says, "There is a better way every day.*
> *How do I find it?" Let's talk about that better way. Let's*
> *look outside. Let's look at other companies. Let's look*
> *everywhere. Then there is this idea to engage people.*
> *Engagement is critical. Get them with a sense of purpose*
> *as to what you are doing, why you are doing it, and*
> *what's in it for them. Is it job security? Is it promotion?*
> *Personal growth? But communicate that to them.*

He especially emphasized the importance of defining "what we are doing and why we are doing it."

John Chambers has an impeccable track record as president and CEO of Cisco Systems, the multinational networking equipment manufacturer that has shown impressive growth since day one—from $2 billion in revenue in 1995 to almost $48 billion in 2014. Reflecting his modesty and humility, Chambers simplified his leading role at Cisco into four functions:

> *I am supposed to do four things reasonably well. The first*
> *is to determine the vision and strategy of my company*
> *based upon the input from my customers and my*
> *leadership team. The second is to develop and recruit*
> *the leaders to implement that vision and differentiated*
> *strategy. The third—and I didn't understand this as a*
> *new business leader—is to develop a culture, and [it]*
> *is such an important part of your success or not as an*
> *organization. And the fourth is to communicate all of*
> *the above. As simple as it sounds, that would be the*
> *scorecard I would use [to evaluate my performance].*

Finally, I'd like to take a look at Google and its research venture Project Oxygen, which aimed to discover the most important elements in successful project management.

In its early years, the basic belief at Google was that great professionals—engineers, software developers—were good bosses. Not surprisingly, Google's leaders soon found out that this was not necessarily the case. So the question came up: What distinguished great bosses from bad ones? In 2009, the tech giant—true to its culture of number crunching—conducted thorough research with its own employees to answer that question.

From that mass of information, Google isolated eight points that make for good leaders:

1. Have a clear vision and strategy for the team.

2. Be a good coach.

3. Express an interest in the team members' success and well-being.

4. Help your employees with career development.

5. Empower your team and don't micromanage.

6. Be a good communicator and listen to your team.

7. Be productive and results-oriented.

8. Have key technical skills so you can help advise the team.

If you look at this list and back at each of the leaders' quotes, you'll notice that several things reappear throughout.

Welch isolates three key leadership roles: first, caring and taking care of people; second, giving the people a sense of purpose or vision; and third, fostering communication. Moreover, through these roles, he highlights the importance of key emotions like fostering engagement and sense of purpose. Chambers echoes those three roles—focusing on the company's vision, people, and communication—but adds a new one: developing a culture. In my opinion the most interesting aspect of his definition of the roles of a CEO are culture and his footnote: *"and I didn't understand this as a new business leader."* There is the pearl! That is his great contribution to a better understanding of leadership! Plus, he highlights culture as the critical variable for the "success or not" of an organization.

The data gathered from thousands of Google surveys, interviews, videos, and performance reviews confirmed that the previously accepted hypothesis was wrong, contradicting the belief that the best leaders are those who have a deep knowledge of the field they work in. Nonetheless, Project Oxygen did not reveal a revolutionary key to management, nor did it produce any kind of modern software to facilitate the work of project managers. Instead, Google's study simply confirmed the most basic but essential concepts of leadership: running an effective management program requires someone who is capable of interacting with people, listening to their concerns, taking care of them, and acting on any information exchanged between the two parties. If we analyze the general conclusions of this project, it is clear that you don't need a divine gift to lead a team. What you really need is a talent for understanding people.

And if we zero in on all the info contained in those five cases, you'll notice a small series of crucial points—first amongst them: people. There is unanimity regarding the importance of your people and attending to them. Both Blair and Powell stress serving followers, while Welch, Chambers, and Google emphasize variously caring about your people, expressing an interest in their well-being, and working to help them develop. Welch is passionate about caring about people and taking care of them. He started the quote talking about people, and he finished it coming back to them. Second, each of our subjects also agrees about the importance of clear vision, mission, and purpose. For Blair, a leader's ultimate role is to provide people with a vision that reflects the truth about the future and to make decisions that he believes will get them closer to that truth. This interest in how decisions are made also informs Google's call to empower your team and not micromanage. Delegating the power to make decisions to team members, then, is key. Finally, Google, Welch, and Chambers all insist on the importance of communication. All of these come down to a leader who creates a culture in which these aspects thrive.

In sketching the contours of the Chief Emotions Officer and the chief roles he plays, I distilled these ideas, reworked them, added my own ideas garnered through personal experience, considered other conversations and studies, and packaged them into something that is my unique conceptualization, my own picture of what an effective leader looks like in the twenty-first century: the Chief Emotions Officer and the five key roles that are the essence of leadership.

THE NEW LEADERSHIP MODEL: FIVE KEY ROLES

The five key roles that make up the essence of leadership and the job of the Chief Emotions Officer are the following:

- Define and ignite the **vision** for the people in the organization.

- Recruit and take care of the **people**, and develop their talent and well-being as much as possible.

- Establish formal and informal systems for people to **communicate** and connect with each other.

- Design a **decision-making** system that empowers people.

- Develop and leverage the appropriate **culture** for the success of the organization.

If we couple this new, specific framework with the model we used earlier in the book, rather than leadership being a general, unspecified umbrella barely balancing out the specific elements of "business-as-usual," we get a fully integrated model that looks like Figure 2.1.

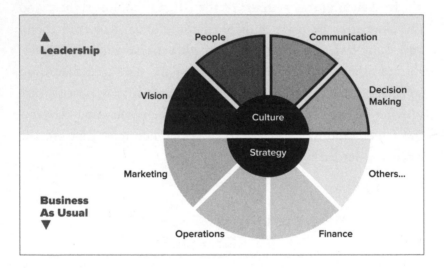

In identifying these five major roles of leadership, my goal is not to pigeonhole them as isolated and perfectly differentiated tasks. Rather, I have chosen to identify each of these functions as a way of simplifying reality so that we can better understand and analyze these roles. Leadership is an incredibly complex and multidimensional phenomenon, and we need to have a comprehensive and integrated outlook on this reality.

You must keep in mind not only that these five key roles are interrelated, but also that it is mainly through these roles that a leader wakes up team members' desirable emotions and states of mind. For example, when a leader establishes the vision (the first leadership role), he gives his team, first and foremost, a sense of purpose; he also gives them a sense of belonging and makes them feel proud. When a leader cares about his people and takes care of them, he lays the ground for a sincere sense of belonging, as well as commitment. The same can be said for the rest of the leadership roles, which all evoke different emotions and states of mind.

Before we look into the skills and qualities a leader needs to better perform her roles, I believe it is important to focus on understanding those roles themselves. Over the next five chapters, we'll look into each one of those leadership roles in great detail and expand on how they generate different positive emotions in the workforce. I am convinced that this will be very useful in helping leaders around the world to improve their personal and team performance.

CHAPTER 3

FIRST ROLE: INSPIRING A VISION

[The people you lead] want to know what the mission is, what you want them to achieve, what the purpose of our operation is. And you, as a leader, have the responsibility to give your followers that sense of purpose, that passion, that intensity. Leaders who are not intense in their beliefs will not cause followers to be intense in their following, so leaders have to be passionate; they have to be intense.

—Colin Powell

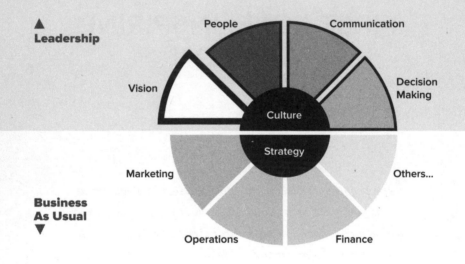

Leadership ▲

Vision

People

Communication

Decision Making

Culture

Strategy

Marketing

Business As Usual ▼

Operations

Finance

Others...

WHAT IS VISION?

Once upon a time in the Middle Ages, a traveler was walking through a village when he came across a man carving stone. Intrigued by the situation, the traveler asked, "What are you doing?" The man replied, "I'm carving stone to make a living and put food on my family's table." The traveler went on his way, and when he came across another worker doing the same job, he asked the question again: "What are you doing?" The second carver answered, "I'm carving a gargoyle, a beautiful, expressive mythological figure." A little more pleased with the second man's purpose, the traveler continued on his way until he came across a third person engaged in the same task as the previous two carvers. The traveler, of course, repeated the question: "What are you doing?" The third man, engaged with his work, answered: "I am building a cathedral."

While the first man is focused on the material value of his work—the food and shelter it provides for him and his loved ones—the second character is focused on the professional and artistic value of his work. Only the third man, however, is able to recognize that his work is part of something bigger and is confident that his daily task is building something more important: *a cathedral*, the architectural miracle of his era, a structure that seeks to unite man with God in all of its beauty.

I first heard this parable when I was working in Paris. I had been living in Paris for almost five years when I received a call from Juan Carlos Villa Larroudet, an Argentine businessman whom I met the following week for dinner. He was building a cathedral, he said.

Like me, he was an engineer and had done an MBA in the United States 25 years earlier, after which he returned to Argentina to found the HMO Omint Group. The company had become one of the top companies in the Argentine healthcare sector and recently expanded to Brazil. He wanted to continue building an innovative company with world-class standards in healthcare and the best service level in Latin America. He wanted to do something great. He wanted to create the future. He wanted to build a cathedral.

I imagined the characters in the parable and was overwhelmingly motivated. Who wouldn't want to work to build a cathedral? It fundamentally alters the world around it—from the landscape and environment to how people relate, act, and go about their daily lives. Who wants to spend his whole life just carving stone when he could be a part of changing reality itself?

After dinner, we were both so excited by this vision for the future and the opportunities for tremendous growth that Villa Larroudet asked me to return to Argentina to work with him, to help him build this cathedral. The story that he shared with me had convinced me to join his team. I accepted his offer and returned to Argentina. A passionate vision is contagious!

As you can guess from this story, establishing a vision is the first fundamental role of the Chief Emotions Officer because vision tells everyone where we are going, the purpose of our job, what we are trying to accomplish, and ultimately what we want to change. The vision provides the road map of the ideas and emotions that we, as a team of people working together to fundamentally alter reality, have to generate and harness to accomplish this objective, to arrive at this new reality. As Anne Mulcahy, former CEO of Xerox Corporation, says, *"A leader must have a clear vision of where she wants the company to go."* Well-known American diplomat Henry Kissinger puts it this way: *"The role of the leader is to get his people from where they are to where they have not been."*

In addition to providing the actual information of the purpose or ultimate goal, by the sheer fact of sharing that vision, of communicating it, of fostering the desire to get there, a leader generates several significant emotions and states of mind: sense of purpose, pride, commitment, passion, and even hope and happiness. It is these emotions that ultimately drive people to work toward the dream or vision.

Vision Is Not Strategy—Vision Is Dream

I suspect that for many of you, this conception of vision has some echoes of strategy, so, before we proceed, let's discuss the relationship between vision and strategy.

We know that the strategy is the guiding principle for all the business variables—marketing, engineering, manufacturing, finance, and so on—and that it pertains solely to the organization's business objectives. While it is true that strategy, business plans, objectives, and specific goals are an effective way of achieving the growth and profits that we are constantly seeking, all of these tools are based in the strategic vision. This is not the same as the leader's vision, which goes way beyond the marketplace. While strategy answers questions like, "In which way are we unique and differentiated compared to our competitors?" "How do we want to compete?" and "What is our competitive advantage?" a leader's vision has to do with people. It has to do with the purpose or dream he sees for his team and the people in his organization, the purpose that gives meaning and identity to a group and motivates them to act to attain their goal. I call this kind of leadership vision *inspirational vision*, and it is obviously very different from the nuts-and-bolts blueprint of strategic vision.

Think about Dr. Martin Luther King Jr., the famous civil rights leader. He didn't say "I have a plan" in his legendary 1963 speech for racial equality, but, rather, he immortalized his fight and vision of life with the famous words, "I have a dream!" In other words, we can think of a leader's vision as the "paradise" where he wants to take the members of his team: it is the dream, the result, what he wants, the ultimate purpose of everything the team does.

Indeed, the most aspirational part of a vision is the dream that inspires it, that place where we most want to go. From a leadership point of view, it could be defined as the goal where all expectations and needs are met. An organization's vision or dream, plus all the emotions and states of mind that will generate its constant pursuit, are the foundations of the organizational culture, and we know the fundamental role of culture in the success of any organization.

Apple's cofounder, chairman, and CEO Steve Jobs, for instance, always understood that much of his company's ability to captivate people around the world was not so much Apple's products themselves or even its marketing strategy. The overwhelming global success of Apple's products, Jobs thought, was due to the company's vision and purpose and the way these were reflected in and embraced by Apple's corporate culture. When Jobs returned to Apple in 1997 after 12 years of absence, realigning vision and culture was exactly where he started. This led to the famous "Think Different" marketing campaign, which reignited the soul and brand of the company. He said at the time: "Our clients want to know who is Apple and what we stand for. Where do we fit in this world. And our *raison d'être* is not building boxes so people can do their jobs—which we are very good at. The heart of Apple, its deep values, are tied to our conviction that people with passion can change this world for good, and we've had the opportunity of working with people like that. . . . And those who are crazy enough to think they can change the world are the ones that end up doing it."[1]

The Relationship Between Vision and Strategy

So, if vision and strategy are generally that different, what is the relationship between a group's strategy and the vision proposed by its leader?

Generally, I would insist that as a leader you need to take a clear and concise strategy and use it to develop a vision that makes the workforce feel passionate and committed to their work. We could think of this leader as a cathedral builder who is able to reach out to his workers and make them feel proud and honored to be participating in the construction of a cathedral. The strategy, the plan, the timetable, all have to do with what actions and tasks have to be performed by whom and when to finish the cathedral that we want. The vision has to do with the aspiration of the individuals who build or will use the cathedral. It might be the dream of accomplishing the unimaginable. The vision is the dream people would like to fulfill, and the role of the leader is to communicate, inspire, and manage this vision, which often means making the individual employee understand that the single stone she is carving is not simply a means to a paycheck or a personally pleasing object, but, rather, one crucial piece in a much larger, extraordinarily significant endeavor. As Jack Welch says: *"Get them with a sense of purpose as to what you are doing, why you are doing it, and what's in it for them."*

In fact, it's important to remember that most great leaders began with small actions and then grew from that starting point. They understood that every action they participated in was part of a bigger dream that went beyond their own personal aspirations, and they were able to communicate this sense of vision to all.

But let's look at this relationship between strategy and vision more concretely by focusing on three specific forms of this relationship: first, a relationship where strategy and vision are allied, but significantly different; second, one where strategy always differs by business unit, but a common vision remains the same and drives the company; third, one where strategy and vision nurture each other and are basically very similar, if not indistinguishable. By exploring these, I hope to elucidate the intimate manner in which strategy and vision are related.

Southwest Airlines is an interesting illustration of a company where strategy and vision are both strong and, while certainly connected, still quite different. Its strategy has always been to provide "low-fare, high-frequency, short-haul, point-to-point service." On the other hand, its vision or ultimate purpose is different: "To connect people to what's important in their lives through friendly, reliable, and low-cost air travel." Its strategy is based on how to compete in the airline business, whereas its vision is what makes everybody jump out of bed every morning and come to work. They are related and consistent, but they are clearly not the same.

Richard Branson's Virgin Group clearly functions differently. Branson once told me that the Group's vision is *"to create a great brand, one that is well respected all over the world, and [to] make a real difference in any new businesses we do."* He elaborated on this by explaining: *"I want people to say, 'Well, that particular sector is not going to be the same again because Virgin went into it.' Our goal is being innovative and making a difference."*

In essence, the Group has to adjust its strategy for each of its many businesses and markets, but its vision always stays the same. Here, we have different strategies across businesses, but a common vision that creates a common culture. This vision of the Group as a brand sets Virgin apart from its competitors and constitutes the basis for its culture.

Similarly to Virgin, Jack Welch's General Electric maintained an overarching, companywide vision, while its individual businesses devised strategies based on their particular markets. When I asked Jack about his original objectives for his first 100 days as CEO of GE upon assuming the post in 1980, he said:

> *I wanted to give us a vision of where we were going. I had a couple of visions about it. I said I wanted to be the number one company in every business—number one and number two—and I wanted to fix, sell, or close every other business, from the broad portfolio of 50 businesses. We have to be the winning company, and I told the people that were going on this journey: "If you do this job, you will have the greatest trip of your life. You will make a lot of money, because I want to make you rich, and I want you to win big and have better lives than you could have ever imagined." And that is what we did. And we fought like hell to make sure they all felt like they were on a winning team.*

With Welch, the driving factor, the purpose that rallied his employees, was not some business strategy; rather, it was a vision, *Jack's* vision, a personal vision that he and his employees would undertake a journey to build a grand company that would enrich everyone's lives, as well as their pockets. It was the ultimate definition of winning. The vision of winning is what drove Jack's dream team at GE. Strategy was a secondary endeavor; in fact, GE didn't have a specific business strategy as a group; strategy was delegated in each one of the multiple businesses, and the group's vision of winning was what propelled its culture and business success.

There are also numerous companies where strategy and vision become nearly indistinguishable. One case that highlights how a strategy can nurture and shape a vision is Natura, a Brazilian cosmetics company whose objective is to create environmentally friendly cosmetics. This goal serves multiple functions: it represents the strategy and value proposition it offers to its clients, as well as the vision the company proposes to its employees. In this case the strategy—how the company competes and differentiates itself—is basically similar to the vision, or the ultimate purpose that drives Natura's employees.

Many NGOs face a similar situation, where their identity is so rooted in their vision that their strategy actually ends up being similar to their vision. For example, the Multiple Sclerosis International Federation is an NGO that seeks to help improve the quality of life for people living with multiple sclerosis and their families. This nonprofit organization's vision and strategy are very similar because its strategic aim is what inspires each of its employees to go to work each day.

VISION INSPIRES EMOTION

What does a leader inspire in his followers when he establishes a vision? Ideally, a vision should generate emotions. As Dave Ulrich, professor of business at the Ross School of Business, University of Michigan, and author, puts it: *"It is not just the motions that we do, but the emotions that we create."* I would argue that the Chief Emotions Officer should focus on inspiring emotions ranging from an absolutely pivotal sense of purpose, belonging, and identity to pride, commitment, a sense of challenge, respect, confidence, hope, happiness, and, crucially, passion. Setting the vision is one of the roles that has a greater impact on inspiring emotions, so I believe it's crucial we spend some time discussing it here.

Although some executives believe that their vision is nothing more than a set of ideas that must be understood and communicated, any vision must go beyond the sphere of ideas. A true vision not only encompasses the ideas that define your purpose, but also has a direct relationship with the emotions and passion that these ideas wake up in each one of your team members. In addition to being conceived, discussed, synthesized, and communicated, provoking interest or disagreement, ideas can evoke passion, anger, joy, sadness, hope, commitment, and an endless number of other emotions and states of mind. These emotions are constantly interacting, leading to new combinations and perceptions—as well as to differing levels of motivation or action. That's why it is so important to understand that vision generates emotions and states of mind that will in turn engender particular behaviors that have a significant impact on attaining results.

Vision Inspires a Sense of Purpose

Leadership requires certain qualities. First of all, vision, and the ability to generate ideas—ideas that would reflect the needs of society at a particular point in time.
—Mikhail Gorbachev,
last head of state of the Soviet Union

An analysis of great leaders' work throughout history reveals how skillfully these characters awoke an emotional response to an idea. Epic leaders propose visions that imply significant changes, but also inspire people to light up emotionally and then work to achieve them. From Mahatma Gandhi looking for Indian independence from the British Empire or Mikhail Gorbachev seeing an end to the Soviet Union to Martin Luther King Jr. dreaming of racial equality, they not only have a political or social proposal or purpose; they get to the hearts of people who become fired up to accomplish it.

Ideas capable of inspiring emotions are an essential part of encouraging people to work toward executing and fulfilling the goals of a project. What is it that makes you jump out of bed to go to work each morning? What makes each member of your team want to do his or her best? It's not just a question of giving them a purpose; it's about giving them an inspiring purpose, one that motivates your team to chase that dream. Indeed, many leadership books refer to motivation but fail to understand that motivation depends on how the vision is formulated. When developing a vision, then, you should include elements that truly motivate people to follow you to the final destination, achieving a greater goal.

Think about the third humble stone carver from the story. He didn't just see his work as a means of earning money or even as an artistic enterprise; rather, he was convinced that he was building something important: a cathedral. Convinced by whom? The architect, local nobleman, or parish priest from whom the vision of the cathedral emanated. Only the architect can produce the blueprints—the strategy and plans—but anyone can provide the vision. And it is the leader's vision that is responsible for generating the energy and sense of purpose that the team needs to build bridges and move mountains in order to accomplish higher goals. Being an effective leader, in large part, has to do with one's ability to help the workforce understand what each one of them wins when they fulfill the vision, thus encouraging them to passionately dedicate themselves to the journey.

Vision Gives the Team a Powerful Identity

Another way of elucidating the fundamental way that a purpose not only motivates people to reach a goal, but also provides them with a greater sense of meaning, pride, commitment, and identity can be found outside the corporate world. While giving a presentation a while ago, I had the opportunity to meet Mario Negri, a famous Argentine rugby player, who illustrated just how important it is to have an identity that serves as the foundation of a strong sense of belonging.

In 1982 two South American teams traveled to South Africa for a rugby tour. The Argentine squad teamed up with Uruguayan, Chilean, and Paraguayan players, and even a Brazilian one, to form the Sudamérica XV "A" and "B" teams. At the time, Mario was not at his best, so the coach decided to take him from the main team and put him on the B team with the rest of the alternates. Mario was upset by the news and hurt by the blow to his pride, but he was still named captain of that team. Unfortunately, the team lacked an identity—or the only identity it had was the uninspiring name "the alternates." I suspect it was hard to rally to a common purpose when the only thing uniting the players was that they were "alternates." How tough is it to get motivated as an alternate? After all, who would want to play on the B team? How do you get people to do their best and play as a team when they are constantly reminded that they are second best?

After a week of training with the A team, Mario Negri and his teammates packed into three trucks and drove to the South African town of Upington, where they were to face the fierce Northwest Cape team. At one point on the lengthy trip, the group stopped at a general store. The Argentine captain went in and found a Foreign Legion kepi, a khaki-colored canvas hat associated with warriors. Mario bought 26, one for each member of the team.

Once they got out onto the field, the Sudamérica XV B team played a very physically, mentally, and emotionally difficult game. However, they won that first match, and the next morning, the local newspaper printed a story about their feat: "The Legionnaires Defeated the Northwest Cape." And just like that, a team and a myth were born.

Thanks to the journalist's creativity, the members of "Sudamérica XV B" ceased to exist, and were replaced by The Legionnaires, a team that, against all odds, won every game and ended the tour undefeated. The A team, on the other hand, lost its first match by a huge difference against the South African selection.

For the A team's rematch against the South African squad, the coaches decided to reinforce it with Negri and four Legionnaires. Mario took on this new role, beaming with Legionnaire pride, and ended up surpassing his coaches' high expectations with a memorable performance that was instrumental in Argentina's historic victory over the South African national team, the formidable Springboks.

The story of Mario and The Legionnaires is an excellent example of how a team can find its identity through external and circumstantial milestones or symbols. The Foreign Legion kepi represented courage to the extreme, and that value gave the players a common identity and, perhaps more important, sparked the emotion to motivate them to victory! Common values, a common purpose or meaning, can help define your identity as a team. You don't have to save the world, or even conquer it. It is enough to have a purpose that unites and motivates your team for you to have a winner.

It's also important to recognize that a team's purpose and identity are complementary. Oftentimes, having a purpose gives you an identity, but having an identity can also give you a purpose. Greenpeace, for example, is an organization whose purpose is to defend the environment, a purpose that gives all of its members an identity and a sense of belonging.

Vision Contributes to Success by Generating Emotion

Vision creates an emotional impact. So far in this chapter, we've seen how vision can be used to motivate people toward a goal by inspiring a sense of purpose, belonging, and identity, but as we mentioned earlier, vision generates numerous emotions, such as pride, commitment, confidence, respect, a sense of challenge, hope, happiness, and passion. Understanding all of these emotions is crucial to building a clear and convincing vision capable of mobilizing the entire company, so let's spend some time exploring them.

I believe *pride* is one of the strongest emotions that a leader can inspire in his team. It is a social emotion. Pride fires you up in relation to the people around you. It makes you ask, "What would my father, mother, or grandmother have said about me?" Pride is the sense that what you are doing is important, that it is valuable not only for you, but in the eyes of society as well. The goal that fosters pride, then, is not a number, such as a 20 percent increase in sales, but a dream that triggers emotions. If the proposed vision is meaningful and aspires to meaningful change, then we will be proud working for such an endeavor.

That's how pride is intimately connected to *purpose*. Purpose adds new meaning, connects people, and brings them together under a common goal. That's why the purpose of a purpose is to create a *shared sense of pride*. If your purpose is true, it will elicit a strong sense of pride among your team, solidifying it, inspiring dedication and effort, and thus improving individual and group performance. That's why purpose is also closely related to commitment.

Commitment has to do with duty. It creates a focused effort to continue working toward the established vision. Indicative of discipline and resilience, commitment means continuing a task even if you are tired or momentarily lack the desire to do it. It has its roots in personal decisions or stands, but it awakens the necessary state of mind to never give up.

I once asked President Clinton who his first mentor was, and he quickly answered, "My mother." When I inquired what he had learned from her, he explained:

> *My mother was a widow three times. My father died before I was born. She had an enormous amount of adversity in her life, and yet she had a good night's sleep every night and got up early every day with a smile on her face and went out to work. She basically taught me that life was a privilege and a gift, and that it had to be enjoyed the most, and that defeats were not permanent unless you gave up, and that bitterness was a foolish feeling, and that no one had a right to any good thing in life, and that basically you should have to go on and never, ever, ever quit. . . . She had an enormous impact on my attitude, and people ask me, "Well, why didn't you quit after you got attacked in 1992?" and I said, "It never even occurred to me. In my family we don't quit."*

That is a huge capacity for commitment!

President Clinton's experiences in 1992 also bring up the relation between commitment and *challenges*. While the challenge he faced was very particular, I think that challenges in general are the result of a desire for improvement and competition. In the conference room or on a sports field, competition and the desire to win are great motivators that release endorphins, as we saw in the previous chapter, and often lead to better performance and self-improvement. Having a challenge is the opportunity to prove to ourselves that we can make it, that we are valuable, and that we can improve our results. When people are challenged, it means that they can feel the energy inside them to work toward the proposed vision. A leader can develop different challenges in each team member to harvest that energy and accomplish the common goal.

Challenging your team to rally toward a common purpose, however, takes more than just the will to do so. It also necessitates *respect*. If a leader has years of training, is qualified, and knows what she is talking about, she will earn the respect of her followers, who will be open to follow her proposed vision. In this regard, Colin Powell says:

> *You don't want them to fear you, but you want them to respect you. You want them to look up to you as a person of the highest standards, who knows what he is doing, that you have prepared yourself; that you know what they are supposed to be doing.*

Respect creates an invisible bridge between the leader and her followers, establishing a mutually beneficial relationship that is strengthened by trust. So a leader can say, "This is possible, and I know how to do it," because she feels confident that her workforce believes in her; they believe that she has the necessary training and judgment to achieve the goals she has set for the team.

In that sense, respect relates to *confidence*. A leader generates confidence in the team—confidence not only in the vision itself, but also that we are moving toward that dream and can ultimately reach it; confidence that pursuing a vision gives our tasks a purpose; and finally, confidence that, once we achieve our vision, each member of the organization will be rewarded.

Yes, an organization's vision or purpose must ensure a concrete benefit for each of its members. Its members must have confidence that they too will benefit—not just senior management. Therefore, if an organization wants to generate the crucial state of mind that is a sense of purpose, it should make sure that achieving that purpose offers its team members benefits, such as being part of something greater than themselves, prestige, higher compensation, or improved levels of personal satisfaction, to name just a few.

Of course, this list of positive emotions is not exhaustive. Depending on the purpose, a leader may inspire *hope* that reality will change and that the team will accomplish the longed-for purpose, and even a certain *happiness* that team members are part of a particular endeavor.

A great vision can also elicit *passion* in your team members. But first, a leader must personally have passion. An effective leader not only gives a dream, a purpose, making a goal meaningful for people, he does so passionately—that is, energetically, with desire, while loving what he does. When one is genuine and truly enjoys one's work, a clear purpose emerges from that passion. Indeed, passion is the result of an internal process that motivates the leader and connects him to his dream or purpose. As we saw, General Powell emphasizes the importance of passion: **"Leaders have to**

be passionate. They have to be intense." If they are not passionate and intense in their beliefs, they won't cause their followers to be! A leader aligns the passion of individuals with the organizational vision. You hire and recruit people that really love what you are trying to achieve.

What you ultimately need to accomplish when setting a vision or a dream is to generate positive emotions such as the ones I've just described. This leads to happier, more fulfilled people, which will enhance individual and group performance and, in the end, generate more successful organizations!

HOW TO MAXIMIZE EMOTION THROUGH VISION

How does one maximize the generation of positive emotions through one's vision? It may seem simple to say, but it is important to realize that setting a vision and a purpose is not just an intellectual exercise. It is not just setting a goal and then "informing" the people about it.

As Anita Roddick, founder of The Body Shop, says, **"People I work with are open to leadership that has a vision, but this vision has to be communicated clearly and persuasively, and always, always with passion."**

Álvaro Uribe Vélez is an excellent example of how a clear, cohesive, and consistent vision and its well-managed communication is powerful enough to implement change—because leadership is about changing reality. Before he was elected president of Colombia in 2002, Uribe was elected governor of Antioquia, one of Colombia's 32 departments and home to its second largest city, Medellín. During his initial post, this amazing leader shaped a concise proposal, which he summarizes like this:

> *I knew that to be able to offer social welfare, we needed investment. And to get investment, we needed security—both legal and physical. So, the three policies that I always proposed as a vision were Security, Promotion of Investment, and Social Welfare. Over time, I realized that the term "security" had negative connotations, so I added the word "democratic": "Democratic security."*

Uribe and his colleagues repeated these concepts over and over again in the media, in interviews, and in front of countless crowds until this leader finally achieved one of his most important accomplishments. **"During the presidential campaign to elect my successor,"** he told me in Buenos Aires in 2009:

> *I came out of a convention center and approached a taxi where the driver was sleeping. I shook him gently to wake him up, and when he saw me, he jumped in his seat and started to say: "Social welfare, investment, and democratic security!" It was so nice to see that the people remembered my message, and that both presidential candidates, from two different parties, had already accepted it as a state policy!*

Summing up this critical idea, I can say that *a vision is what I get when I visualize my goal, and then boil it down to a sentence that makes it easier for my team to understand and get fired up to execute.*

As the Uribe example makes clear, it's not just that a leader needs to have a pithy, easy-to-understand vision; it is equally important that a leader has and expresses a clear and *consistent* vision—one in line with overall strategy. Guy Kawasaki, former chief evangelist of Apple, entrepreneur, and author, makes this point by stressing what he calls *mantra*. In his opinion, if a company wants to ensure that its mission and strategic vision are truly implemented within the organization, the leadership must clearly and concisely communicate consistent guiding principles in a way that is easy for the workforce to understand—the mantra.

Kawasaki, considered partially responsible for Apple's comeback, has criticized, for example, the mantra of the fast-food chain Wendy's, which, he argues, defines its purposes using a language that is alien to the nature of its business: "Our guiding mission is to deliver superior-quality products and services for our customers and communities through leadership, innovation and partnerships." During an onstage conversation I had with Kawasaki in 2013, he explained that Wendy's fails to convey its strategic goals with this mantra. On one hand, it is really not specific to its business, to the way the company wants to compete and differentiate itself; on the other, it is so lengthy and full of jargon that it wouldn't be easily understood by or inspiring to anyone in the organization or the customers beyond. So, he proposed a different mantra: "Healthier fast food." He concluded that ***"the company could use these three simple words to more clearly and acutely communicate its vision to both its workforce and the millions of consumers who visit Wendy's restaurants each day."***

The clarity and consistency of your vision is without a doubt central, but, as we discussed earlier, it is crucial that your vision have emotional reach so that it can inspire and excite people. It is not enough for your workforce to understand the goal on an intellectual level; they must also get it on an emotional level in order for you to win their commitment and determination. The emotions you awaken in your people really matter!

WHAT DO I NEED TO CREATE
AND IMPLEMENT A VISION?

To generate the necessary emotions in other people, you need to feel them yourself first. That is, in order to even feel those emotions, you first have to have personal awareness of your dreams and values and, second, work for an organization whose vision is compatible with those personal dreams and values. So, on the one hand, you need thorough personal awareness in order to know your own dreams and values and to propose them to others, and, on the other, you need to find an organization that proposes a vision compatible with your personal dreams and values so that you can join it and work passionately and with commitment to achieve that vision.

Know Yourself and Believe in the Vision

Rudy Giuliani, mayor of New York City during the September 11 attacks, says:

> *The first and most important principle of leadership is: "To be a leader you have to have strong beliefs; you have to know what you believe; you have to know what you stand for."*

Before I can begin to lead a large number of people, I must identify my talents, my passions, my desires, and my interests. I must know the answers to the most personal questions: Who am I? What impact do I want to have on the world? What are my core values (those that genuinely determine my choices)? What is my dream? It's important for all of us to reflect on the convictions, values, and ideas that drive us in our roles as leaders, to ask ourselves, "What are my deepest beliefs? What is the vision I most passionately wish to pursue?" The quest for these answers is a long journey that we must take one step at a time.

We will discuss this in much more detail in Chapter 8, but, for now, it's important to stress how this self-knowledge promotes internal motivation, which is absolutely key to the creation and pursuit of vision and dreams. For instance, in a 2014 *Harvard Business Review* article, Tom Kolditz shares the results of thorough research showing that leaders with intrinsic motivations have better leadership abilities that those with external motives, such as compensation, promotion, or the like. What was surprising, however, was to find "that those with *both* internal and external rationales proved to be *worse* investments as leaders than those with fewer, but predominantly internal motivations. Adding external motives didn't make leaders perform better—additional motivations reduced the selection to top leadership by more than 20 percent. Thus, external motivations, even atop strong internal motivations, were leadership poison."[2] The point here is that internal motivation fuels the best leaders, so a strong leader must without exception have both internal motivation and knowledge of her internal motivations. If I know myself, I'll understand what it is I want to do—what I really love and dream of doing—and why I want to pursue those things. I'll be able to gauge my talents and my weaknesses, as well as know how to accept them and be open to learning and growth. This will all help drive me at the same time as it makes me able to deal with change.

I'd like to offer my own personal story here as an example of how a lifetime journey of knowing yourself and what you love can spark the internal motivation to help you both formulate your personal vision and aid yourself in its pursuit.

I come from a family where having a dream, as well as the commitment, pride, and passion to attain that vision, has always been very important, and this history has affected and shaped me in profound ways.

Mauricio Braun, my great-grandfather, arrived on the shores of Punta Arenas in the Strait of Magellan in 1874, when he was only eight years old. When he was 22, he started working as a clerk for an already successful immigrant, Jose Menendez, and soon proved to be a very smart young man. He partnered in some small businesses with his boss and was soon creating companies in different sectors and growing his fortune. At the age of 29, he married his boss-partner's daughter, Josefina Menendez, and went on to create one of the biggest empires in Patagonia, spanning millions of acres of land with sheep and forming a trading company to export wool to England, a supermarket chain, a ship company, and one of the first Argentine airlines. With the building of the Panama Canal, the region gradually lost the maritime traffic between the Atlantic and the Pacific, and he finally decided to move to Buenos Aires in 1916, at the age of 50. By then he had 11 sons and daughters, one of whom had my father, the eldest grandson of Mauricio Braun's 65 grandchildren.

Since I was born, I have looked up to my father, who worked for the family business for 40 years—something I always imagined that I would one day do. Toward that purpose, I studied in the rigorous six-year industrial engineering program at the University of Buenos Aires. Then, in order to be ready to cope with the challenge of managing a large company, I dreamed of going to the United States to do an MBA at the Wharton School.

Studying abroad at a top-tier school, however, was prohibitively expensive. I was now married and economically independent, but my salary as a full-time engineer was the equivalent of $3,600 USD a year. So the chances of saving enough money to make it to Wharton were slim—to say the least!

I started exploring any options I could find. Plus, I started preparing a big art exhibition. Yes, at the age of 13 I had begun taking watercolor painting lessons with one of the best Argentine painters. After nearly 10 years of classes and an apprenticeship in Paris to perfect my painting, I won a couple of national awards, as well as two international prizes, and was able to organize a massive exhibition and sell my paintings quite well. By also winning three different scholarships, I was able to secure most of my first year's tuition. So I went to ask my dad for the remaining expenses, and he proudly consented after the commitment I'd shown to my goal.

After the first year, I worked a summer job for Booz Allen & Hamilton in Brazil and Argentina. It was June and July 1989, and Argentina had 200 percent monthly inflation! Local prices were so low in dollar terms that I was able to save almost all three months of my salary. When Booz Allen offered to take care of my second year of tuition if I would return to work for them after graduation from Wharton, I couldn't say no!

I was excited at the prospect of working for Booz Allen after graduation, but I had my sights set on horizons other than Argentina or Brazil. I asked if I could go to work for the company in Paris, where I had great memories from my painting atelier, and enough French to work my way through. Booz decided to give me the opportunity and flew me to Paris for interviews with its local partners on November 9, 1989. It was the day of the fall of the Berlin Wall. The world had changed fundamentally and was beginning a new era. I was, too.

After a whole day of interviews at the Paris offices, I received an offer to work for them. The total package for the first year was almost $105,000 USD! I left the office around 7 p.m. and started walking around the streets of Paris, feeling, I imagine, like Aristotle Onassis when he earned the money to buy his first ship. I was going to make 30 times more than before Wharton!

I graduated in May 1990, and was off to Paris, where I worked very hard at Booz Allen, learning an enormous amount as Europe looked forward to December 1992 and the creation of a single market. It was such an exciting time to be in Europe, working to build that future! In fact, it was such an exhilarating time that I was faced with a new choice: return home to the family business and my childhood dream or, like Europe, set out on a new course and pursue a new dream, something on a grander scale that needed to be found elsewhere. I realized that I needed to readjust my personal vision and find a larger purpose again. I needed to change my reality.

Recognize on a Personal Level That You Can Change Reality

Steve Jobs has said that the secret to life is realizing one's own potential to make a difference: "Once you discover one simple fact—that everything around you that you call 'life' was made up by people that were no smarter than you—the minute you understand that, that you can change life, you can mold it, that's maybe the most important thing. Once you learn that, you'll never be the same again."[3]

Many people believe that reality is a box we have to fit into, a place where we have to comply with norms and complete whatever work is assigned to us. Most people take reality as a given: things are the way they are, and they can't be changed. Generally, humans tend to feel that they are victims of big changes and other people's decisions, failing to acknowledge their own autonomy and responsibility in making their reality and deciding how it will evolve. Each one of us has the possibility to change our reality, both in our direct surroundings and in our broader environment. So, once you have recognized that you have the ability to modify your own environment and alter your possibilities, you will make a quantum leap as a leader. Leadership is about changing reality in some way, so setting the vision is explicitly recognizing that you can change reality, and clearly stating in which ways you want to do so.

Understand Your Surroundings

As a leader, once I've understood myself, my vision, and that I can indeed change reality, I must work toward implementing that vision. In order to do this, I must also understand my surroundings.

Perhaps the first thing you need to realize in this is that you are not alone, so listening and understanding what the people you lead want and the context in which all this takes place is very important. I once asked Felipe González, prime minister of Spain from 1982 to 1996, if a true political leader is one who chooses a direction and then tries to convince the people to follow him, or if it is one who understands what the people want and then proposes that same direction. He replied to my question with a smile, "Well, it's a bit of both." A leader not only selects what he wants and then works hard within the company to get his team to achieve his goal; as we will see in the following chapter, he listens to his team and their aspirations and dreams. A true leader will balance his vision and values with an analysis and understanding of his surroundings.

Indeed, understanding your surroundings in terms of politics, work, and culture is essential to establishing a more balanced vision. Leaders who understand what is at stake in a moment in history are the ones capable of defining an appropriate vision. An effective leader has to know how to read his reality and understand the current situation. He will sense which direction the world is moving in, what needs to be changed, and what he wants changed.

But once I've understood my surroundings and analyzed the prospects for change, I have to decide what I think, what values I stand for, and how I should act on them. Is this difficult to do? Of course it is! It's almost impossible! Nonetheless, we must always keep the vision in mind, remain deeply convinced of it, and understand the context so that we can better achieve that dream. This awareness is not only a decisive factor throughout life, but also an "acid test" for leaders like Jack Welch, who said:

> *In a crisis, you have to understand what you stand for, what is your purpose and which are your personal values.*

Indeed, once you know what you want for yourself, what you believe, what you want to achieve, and what your surroundings are—that is, as soon as you know your vision and find the emotional resources necessary to pursue it—it is easier to create an organization to get there or join one that already exists.

Why Is It So Hard for Us to Work on a Vision?

Though I insist that emotion is the overall key for successful leadership and of the utmost importance in the formulation and pursuit of vision, emotion can sometimes get in the way of vision. In fact, we have to ask: If vision is so crucial to success, why do such a large percentage of people fail to set their own vision? There are many reasons for ignoring your personal and professional vision of life, but perhaps one of the most common is fear. For instance, I become terrified when I think that I may not achieve what I set out to do, and so I prefer to sit still and stay silent. We're all afraid of establishing an overly ambitious vision and not being able to fulfill it, because, ultimately, you will have to look inside and ask, "Did I give my absolute best to get there?" You'll also have to evaluate if it was enough or not. It is tough to say that you really wanted something and gave your best to get it, and then realize that it was far from enough.

You Don't Have to Be CEO

Beyond fear, another excuse often used to avoid setting an ambitious vision is to repeat to yourself that you are not the CEO, that you're not in charge and that it is not your job or responsibility: "I would set this or that vision, but it is not my job. It's the CEO's."

But do you necessarily have to be a CEO to establish a vision and inspire your team? Although defining the overall vision and setting the road map to achieve it are key responsibilities of the leader, we can all propose more modest visions and try to convince our peers. Moreover, visions or dreams are "nested," in the sense that your small team can have a vision that is consistent and contributes—together with the rest of the small teams—to the whole organization's dream. So, no, you don't have to be a CEO to establish a vision and inspire your team. To be honest, you don't even have to be a boss to inspire with your vision; you simply have to be a member of the team. As Nando Parrado, former rugby player and survivor of the Uruguayan Air Force flight that crashed in the Andes Mountains in 1972, insists: *"Leadership evolves with a situation, not because anyone wants to become a leader. Leaders evolve because of the situation."*

Perhaps you are part of an organization that lacks a vision, where you are just given a couple of goals. Well, go ahead and transform those goals into a vision for your department. Think about new ways of accomplishing the team's objectives and create a specific project based on those goals so that your team gets inspired. By identifying an important challenge or a specific learning experience, you can start creating a new "team spirit" that will lead to a new course of action.

Defining a vision is part of a learning process, and as you become more confident throughout your career, the "visions" that you set for yourself and your team will grow and will probably be more ambitious and more in line with your own personal dreams. As a result, your leadership capacity will grow over time, too.

So, I'd like to invite you—whether you are the worker carving a single stone for building the cathedral or the architect of the building, whether you're an entrepreneur, an executive, a manager, or another employee—to recognize your role as a leader in society—whether you like it or not—and to take a stand, not only in the professional world, but also in the public sphere. Wherever you are, however high up you are in your organization, take this challenge and start the leadership process right now! It's all about people. It's all about you!

Remember, *an organization's vision or dream, plus the emotions that it generates, are the foundation of any organization's culture.* Or, to put it another way, culture's first pillar is the vision that drives it, and, as we've seen, culture is fundamental to the success of any organization. To check if you, as Chief Emotions Officer, are leveraging this role of creating vision, I invite you to ask yourself the following questions:

What is your dream? What is the organization's dream?

CHAPTER 4

SECOND ROLE: BEING ALL ABOUT PEOPLE— YOUR PEOPLE!

The business of business is people. It's all about people. . . . People are the only sustainable competitive advantage a business has.

—Herb Kelleher

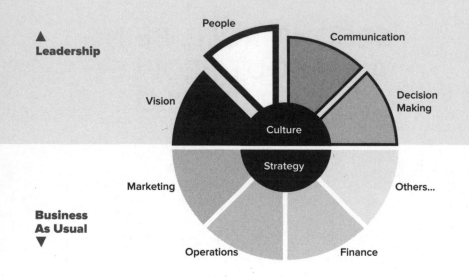

Leadership ▲

People

Communication

Decision Making

Vision

Culture

Strategy

Others...

Marketing

Business As Usual ▼

Operations

Finance

FROM A GOOD LEADER TO
A GREAT LEADER

If you are a leader, you have to understand implicitly,
deep in their souls, the importance of other people. You
can never think the world revolves around you.
—**Rudy Giuliani**

The second key leadership role is to focus on people. This includes not simply assembling the best possible team you can, but also, once you have found those people, genuinely caring about and taking care of them. Good leaders recognize that they need people in order to achieve success. After all, without a strong team, without people, no one can do anything significant. Management expert and bestselling author Ken Blanchard puts it succinctly: **"People are not the most important resource of your organization, they are your organization. When they go home, you've got nothing."** However, what distinguishes *great* leaders—and the Chief Emotions Officer—is that they also deeply and genuinely care about their people and then take good care of them.

Deeply and genuinely caring about people has a profound effect on the organization as a whole because how leaders *care about* and *take care of* their people will be reflected in the organizational *values*, a fundamental element that makes up an organization's culture. The leader's behavior is a reflection of the values undergirding the culture, so, in the way a leader assembles and treats his people, we see whether the organization tends to view its people more as human resources or as human beings. This, too, has extraordinary consequences on the organization and its level of achievement. As in the case of setting the vision, when you genuinely care about and take care of the people you have chosen as your team, you awaken a series of very important emotions in your team members, such as *a sense of belonging, a sense of community, pride, engagement, commitment,* and *trust.* As we saw in the prior chapter, these emotions are very important to enhancing performance.

ASSEMBLING AND DEVELOPING A TALENTED TEAM

The most valuable property is talent.
—**José Mujica,** president of Uruguay, 2010–2015

I never thought running an organization would be so complex. I have learned, however, that it's all about people—getting the right people. . . . Talent is the number one priority for a CEO.
—**Andrea Jung,** former CEO of Avon,
president and CEO of Grameen

If people are the key to your success as a leader, then your first step is obviously to assemble a team of the very best people you can get your hands on. In his excellent book *Great People Decisions,* longtime headhunter Claudio Fernández-Aráoz identifies the ability to make great people decisions as the single most powerful contributor to career success:

Once you are a manager, nothing is more important than making great people decisions because everything will depend on the people you've chosen—you do everything through others. Making the great people decision is even more important than having the right strategy; the right people will help you define the right strategy and implement it, but it doesn't work the other way round.

More important, he argues that, beyond following a highly disciplined search process, being able to assess and understand people enough to make the right decisions concerning their appropriateness for your team is a craft that can be learned.

Leaders Assemble the Best Team by Recruiting the Best People

If talent is key to attain success in your organization, then you need to recruit the best talent. So, how do we build the best possible team? There are obviously many dimensions to what "best talent" is. Just think back to Tony Hsieh's story! But one of the most compelling things I've noticed about the recruiting practices of the most accomplished leaders is that they focus on people who are better than they are—that is, people who possess greater surpluses of the qualities that they themselves have.

For example, great leaders love hiring intelligent people, but, interestingly, they are particularly keen to seek out people who are even more intelligent than they are. Jack Welch, for one, insists, *"Don't be the smartest person in the room."* In fact, he says that a key to his successful career was to always be surrounded by the best professionals. *"I love smart people. I look for smart people and the type of person that, as well as being smart, has the courage and confidence in his convictions. I look for people that accept the challenge and fight tirelessly,"* says Welch.

Former Spanish prime minister Felipe González agrees whole-heartedly with this opinion. He says that, in order to take full advantage of the intellectual capital and innovative minds out there, you have to work with geniuses, although this may mean *"putting up with brilliance, which can be quite bothersome."* González admits that managing brilliance in a human team can be difficult, but, he insists, *"failing to take advantage of it is stupid."*

More generally, Andrea Jung and Carl Icahn both look for people who possess or can develop characteristics that they might not actually have and that they might wish to emulate. Jung explains, *"Spend the time to ask yourself who you can get who can be better than you."* The corporate raider and Icahn Enterprises founder puts it this way: *"It's better to hang out with people better than you. Pick out associates whose behavior is better than yours."*

Leaders Are Resourceful in Building Their Teams in Consideration of Limitations

Great leaders strive to hire the best talent, but they are also great at identifying the talent available to them within the particular limits of their circumstances. That is the case of Jean-Claude Biver, CEO of the Swiss watch company Hublot. In 2004, Biver took over the company, which was in critical condition: it had about 20 employees, less than $25 million in annual sales, and, according to Biver, three-quarters of the company was bankrupt.

What was he to do in the face of such an outlook? Well, Jean-Claude, a longtime executive in the watch industry, analyzed the situation: *"We wanted the best team because only with the best team could we reconquer the world, but, unfortunately, we could not afford it."* So he thought up another solution: recruiting retirees.

Wow! In Switzerland and all over the world, many 62- or 65-year-olds are pushed into retirement because they are seen as too old to work, but Jean-Claude refused to accept this, explaining: *"Your age is not in your passport. Your real age is in your brain, in your eyes, in your heart, in your blood, and in your passion."* He immediately hired a team of retirees with enviable experience and an enormous potential for production at a very low cost: *"A 67-year-old production manager, a 69-year-old purchasing manager, a 71-year-old sales director, a metallurgical expert that was 74—suddenly we were the best team of the past to conquer the future,"* he said. Jean-Claude Biver had identified and recruited available talent and given them a very powerful identity: "The best team of the past to conquer the future!"

And so it was! In just three years, sales at Hublot grew by 500 percent, reaching almost $130 million in revenues. At that point Biver sold the company to the luxury goods group LVMH for an unrevealed amount that was certainly a big win for Biver. As this case shows, knowing how to build a team with the best talent your circumstances permit is essential. Moreover, it suggests that bringing out the best in your talent is equally crucial because all members of your team are valuable.

Leaders Realize the Value of Team Members and Bring Out Their Best

> *I've learned that leaders must inspire everyone*
> *they touch to be the best they can be.*
> —**Kevin Roberts,** CEO Worldwide of Saatchi & Saatchi

A team leader is seldom able to build the dream team, and any group will always have a few less talented members. I've heard many executives use this as an excuse: "I can't fulfill my objectives because I didn't assemble my team. The people I have here are no good." However, all team members are valuable in their own way; you just need to know how to bring out the best in them and develop their talents.

One way to do this is to make sure that every person is working at what she does best every day. As business management expert Tom Peters says, *"Happiness is when you are able to develop your personal skills to an enormous degree."* A leader is responsible for this because it can often be not just the difference between happy and disgruntled or underfulfilled employees, but also between success and failure. Best known for promoting the idea that people should focus on leveraging and developing their strengths rather than offsetting their weaknesses, international bestselling author and business consultant Marcus Buckingham says:

> *All a great company is is a deliberate accumulation of lots and lots of great teams. That's what makes a great company. So we've got to know what the difference is within a company, what creates the difference in performance. If you have but one question to distinguish the overperforming from the underperforming teams, the question I would ask is, "At work, do you have the opportunity to do what you do best every day?" That isn't the only question you should ask, but it is the most important.*

Don't underestimate this idea that the differentiating factor between over- and underperforming teams has to do with permitting your team members to do what they do best every day. Gary

Hamel points out some *"fundamentally scandalous"* data: *"maybe only 10 or 20 percent of the people in the economy are highly engaged."* Peters echoes this, citing a 2005 Gallup study asserting that "55 percent of the U.S. workforce is 'actively disengaged' in their work at an annual productivity cost of $328 billion."[1] Hamel posits as one reason for this that the management models used by most companies nowadays are models inherited from the Industrial Revolution—and consequently based on outdated premises. Back then, companies were designed to produce goods on a large scale in order to reduce costs and gain access to mass markets, which forced them to standardize products, together with their operations and production processes. Furthermore, tasks had to be simple and repetitive because a large majority of the workforce was illiterate.

The growing emergence of services and, in particular, custom-made services has required companies to look in a different direction. Today's service, knowledge, and creativity economy no longer needs obedient workers to complete constant and repetitive tasks, but, rather, an intelligent and educated workforce capable of making decisions and taking advantage of their ability to interact with others. Hamel says:

Human beings are just innately creative, have a right to be creative; yet there are so many things in an organization that work against this. I am heavily influenced by data that basically shows how disengaged people are in their work, how little of their emotion and their passion and creativity they bring to work every day. And I think that if you are a manager and you see that data—that maybe only 10 or 20 percent of the people in the economy are highly engaged—it's just fundamentally scandalous.

In short, simple repetitive tasks are not what your workforce can do best each and every day. You need to capture the innate passion and emotion of your team members; you need to develop their creativity. When you don't make good use of the intelligence and creativity of the workforce, you spoil its talent. When you don't fully use the minds of your people, you actually don't get their passion and emotions either! You get disengagement and underperformance. One of your major roles as leader, then, is to harness what people do best and develop their innate talents and characteristics so that you get the very best out of everyone.

Leaders Are Always Developing People

A leader must be an expert in managing talents. If the leader is not capable of understanding talent, if he doesn't understand how to use talent, how to nourish talent, how to employ talent, then that person is an analyst, not a leader.

—**Ram Charan,** world-renowned business advisor and author; Distinguished Fellow of the National Academy of Human Resources

I always look for leaders that are passionate about developing talents and unleashing the potential in people. That's the greatest joy in business.

—**Carly Fiorina**

To me, Fiorina's comment is incredibly important. Isn't the joy of business the essence of deeply and genuinely caring for people, looking out for their personal and professional growth, and passionately laboring to develop their innate talent?

Muhammad Yunus, Nobel Peace Prize winner and founder of Grameen Bank, a microfinance organization and community development bank, shared with me an amazing example of this concept of developing the talent innate in everyone. Yunus faced harsh criticism from many sectors of society when he created a bank to offer microloans to the poorest of the poor. His critics claimed that only people with special entrepreneurial talent should receive such aid. Yunus, who was convinced otherwise, devoted himself to proving that all human beings are entrepreneurs and that this trait is not limited to a small percentage of society. In his opinion, some people discover their entrepreneurial ability, while others do not. His goal was to give people the opportunity to develop their personal initiatives and potential.

As a way of proving the idea that microcredits were "only for entrepreneurs" wrong, Yunus reached out to to beggars with his microcredits. During one conversation, he told me:

So one way we wanted to demonstrate it was by giving loans to beggars, and if beggars can find their own talent and be creative, that will show that even the beggars can be creative entrepreneurs. So we started talking to the beggars, and the idea that we promoted was that, "As you go from house to house begging, would you carry some merchandise with you? Some cookies, some candies or some toys for the kids, so that the people that you meet in the house have some options?" . . . Now we have more than 100,000 beggars and many of them have left the streets completely. We started four years ago, and, today, more than 11,000 people are no longer asking for free money, while the rest are beggars and part-time salespeople.

What a fantastic experience! Allowing thousands of outcasts to fend for themselves and make a living. Helping them to change their realities and counteract prejudice with a big dose of self-esteem. So, after seeing Yunus's powerful results with beggars, how can CEOs argue that they are unable to do anything with an "average" employee?

Leaders Help Create Leaders, Not Followers

The old paradigm was that leaders would create followers, while the new paradigm is that leaders should produce new leaders.
—**Stephen Covey,** writer, keynote speaker,
and Doctor of Religious Education

In one way, we could argue that Yunus created beggars who became CEOs, leaders of their own companies. Perhaps this is an extreme example, but I don't think it's far-fetched to say that this is indeed the ultimate goal. In an ideal world, the talent you hire and develop would become the next leaders. When you develop your team and bring out the best in each person, you are not only helping them find and develop their talents, you are also helping them find their own voice, what they want to do in life, how they want to change the world. Ultimately, this results in finding the leader inside them and bringing it out. Great leaders are those who, instead of attracting followers, work to create new leaders.

Leaders Know Their Team Members to Identify Talent and Develop Leadership Qualities

So how do you do all of this? In order for a leader to get the most out of the talent she has found, to get the most out of the team she has assembled and to develop new leaders down the road, she needs to identify what each person does best and what he enjoys doing, the worker's talents and passions. OK, but how does one identify these things?

The key to successfully doing this is getting to know your employees, and in order to accomplish that, you need to learn to ask questions about, listen to, and observe and understand even the subtlest aspects of their behavior. In the end, you need to see your employees less as resources and more as people. You need to really care about them as people and not only as employees.

LEADERS CHAMPION HUMAN VALUES

Before I elaborate on the need to see employees less as human resources and more as human beings, I think it's important to understand the important role of values and behaviors in underlying how we see our employees, how we treat them, and how we care about them. So, please allow me to take a moment here to talk a bit about values and behaviors and the distinction I wish to draw between them, although most executives do not make a distinction. For Jack Welch, for example, values and behaviors are interchangeable, whereas Tony Hsieh labels everything under these rubrics as values. I think that distinguishing them is quite useful because it allows us to choose and manage each element properly.

In an organization's culture, every value turns into a behavior, so we could actually talk about pairs of "value-behaviors." For instance, the value "humbleness" goes hand-in-hand with the behavior of "being able to ask for help." Moreover, you will always have several behaviors for a given value, so the value "humbleness" also elicits behaviors such as "saying I don't know" and even "recognizing others."

All behaviors have values behind them, and values are always expressed in behaviors. If you think about it, a value is transformed into a behavior when a decision is made. For example, if we establish "honesty" as a value, it will be manifested in decisions that result in a number of specific behaviors, such as "not bribing" or "not using defective materials in the manufacturing process."

Over the course of the rest of the book, I will refer to those value-behavior pairs that relate to people as "values" and those value-behavior pairs that relate to the business as "behaviors." Therefore, when I speak of values, please keep in mind that these are value-behavior pairs that have to do with human beings, with people (how they are perceived, the vision or ideals they hold dear, etc.). When I refer to behaviors, please know that I am discussing value-behavior pairs that are more related to business (the necessary attitudes to deliver the value proposition, etc.). This is also why I often add the adjective *strategic* and talk of *strategic behaviors*—to make it clear that they are our link to our strategy, to the value proposition of the business.

It is important to note that, as values have to do with one's vision regarding people, a large variety of companies and sectors may share the same values; behaviors, however, are clearly related to the company's strategy and, therefore, can evolve over time or even have different applications in different sectors of the company (different subcultures), as I will explain later.

Simply put, though, the values of a company determine how people are treated, how they are cared for, and the forms and shapes those behaviors take. Behaviors like praise and recognition, bringing out the best in people, creating leaders and not followers, all show that people and the way we treat them are a priority—that they are *valued*. Those behaviors and the corresponding set of values behind them are then identified, communicated, and implemented, and this multiplies individual and group performance.

Along with the organization's vision and dream, these values are a second pillar supporting an organization's culture.

I know that this may come across as a cliché, but it isn't. If we say that human beings are the starting point of culture, we must then choose which values we believe in and are willing to put into practice. The scale of values is responsible for establishing the basic, invisible rules that will govern the relationship between employees and their company, and the professional priorities—the actual behaviors that come to pass. Plus, this implicit code of conduct gets reflected in the personnel policies and corporate decisions in general.

An extreme but very illustrative example of this concept is the armed forces. For an armed forces member, obeying orders and successfully completing missions—behaviors—are more important than that person's life. Indeed, soldiers have to prioritize obeying orders, even if their own lives are at risk.

Luckily, the business world does not expect such a high level of commitment from its workers. However, just like the strong relationship between the military institution and its members, the interaction between a company and its workers is a reflection of the company's values. For example, according to Herb Kelleher, if someone at Southwest Airlines was in mourning, everyone else was, as well, and the same thing happened with joy and celebration, thus putting empathy above the company's goals. When caring about people is a value above and beyond business results, it shows in every business decision and every behavior.

And because an organization takes note of the values and behaviors of leaders above anyone else, as a leader you have to explore what your value scale is, both for yourself as a leader and for your company. Furthermore, since it's called a scale, you also have to determine which values are ranked higher on the list. In particular, you must decide what is more important—a person's work or his personal life?

Moreover, you'll have to consider what happens when these values conflict. If one of my employees comes and tells me that his godson is getting married the following afternoon, should I let him go? Under what conditions? Are these answers applicable to a father who wants to attend his child's school performance? What if his child is sick? How does the company react? How should the company proceed under even more complex circumstances—for example, when an employee feels ill, but has a major presentation tomorrow? In that case, where do the company's priorities lie?

A company and its leaders must also choose between trusting people and controlling employees, between exploiting them and developing them. Does the company think that people are mature enough to motivate themselves in a setting with lots of freedom and little outside control? Or conversely, should employees be placed under lots of control, with little freedom? Are the company's employees capable of working in a flexible structure that allows them to organize their own schedules, or do they need to comply with a strict calendar? Will they be allowed to work from home under certain conditions? Does the company want people to enjoy their time at work, or is it simply interested in the group's productivity? Should group work be competitive or cooperative? Do team members trust each other?

I'm certain that each of you has your own position on each of these questions. That's great. It's indispensable to remember that you need to have a stance on these situations because your stance defines the general values of the company. Through these choices you and the company establish a clear moral contract and set of values by which the employees are expected to live or behave. Through them, each worker, consciously or unconsciously, will know what the "implicit contract" with the organization is and consequently how to behave.

Leaders Recognize That People Are Not Resources, but Human Beings

I really think that our humanistic approach to our people was probably more essential than anything else, because we value them as individuals, not just as workers. We pay an enormous amount of attention to them. We grieve with them when they have some unfortunate event in their personal life. We rejoice with them when they have something in their personal life that is a source of joy. We try to make our people aware of the fact that we value them as people, not just as workers.
—**Herb Kelleher**

I'm not a human resource. I think it's a human insult to call you . . . resource, so don't call me human resource. I'm a human being. You're a human being. We're people. So they say, "What are we going to call the department?" I say, "It's a People Department." Call it "The Human Being Department." . . . "Human resources" is a terrible term. Just think about it: we're resources, a human asset or human capital. [It] is this economic domination of our thinking that's horrible.
—**Henry Mintzberg,** internationally renowned academic and author

Despite the recognition that "it's all about people," very few companies and executives actually treat their employees as though they were real, living human beings with wants, needs, feelings, and lives outside the office. Instead, employees are most frequently used and valued as "human capital," "human resources"—impersonal tools, cogs on a wheel or interchangeable workers on an assembly line. This is deeply embedded in business culture and takes its most obvious—and farcical—form in the title "Human Resources," given to the department most broadly charged with managing people, their recruitment, their development, their performance appraisal, and so on. As Mintzberg explains, the very term posits people less as human beings than as assets, tools, or capital.

It's not hard to imagine how valuing and treating people as human beings rather than as resources or capital may lead to greater success. Bill Conaty was Jack Welch's senior vice president of human resources—what a paradox that they still used that name!—for nearly 15 years. The secret of his success was deeply caring about people and considering them as human beings. Conaty told me:

> *I had a boss at GE. It wasn't Jack Welch; it was someone before Jack who said, "This is the first human resources guy that ever worked for me that really cares about human beings."*

This does indeed also explain why Conaty worked so well with Jack to lead the "people side" of General Electric. Jack talks about companies by focusing on people. In fact, he talks about corporations *as* people. They are human beings, not resources, not buildings, not assets, and so you have to care about them:

> *Corporations are people—they have sorrows; they have losses. . . . Many want to demonize them because they see them like they were buildings, but they are more like communities. . . . Each one is a family, and they take care of one another. You may ask them to*

> *leave if they are not delivering results; if they are, you may reward them, but they are all human beings.*

Kelleher also created a culture in which employees were valued as human beings and encouraged to act like them, rather than as faceless resources or exchangeable capital. He explains:

> *We value the people in our organization. We ask them to be themselves, to have the liberty to be themselves at work. We say, "We didn't hire you because you're an automaton or a robot; we hired you because of your personality, so continue to be you at work." . . . They can have fun; they can be creative; they are given a great deal of latitude as to what they may face.*

From a Customer-First Model to an Employee-First Model

One aspect of how employees are treated that has changed radically in some companies has to do with how they are viewed in relation to the customers they are there to serve. In order to understand this, let's take a look back at the dual framework I introduced in Chapter 1. In the "business-as-usual" system, which emphasizes hard variables, the customer is the most important factor, and that has been the motto over the past few decades:

- "Put the customer first!"

- "The customer is always right!"

- "Always give the customer more than she expects. Surprise her!"

- "Never underestimate the power of an angry customer!"

But when we add that invisible layer called leadership to this system, it gives us a whole new perspective, and it becomes clear that the most important factor in my organization is the people who work in it. I will only be able to serve my customers with our products and services—and thus earn money—if I have a trained, respected, emotionally developed, and energetic workforce by my side.

That's why, without hesitation, Southwest's Kelleher says,

> *Employees and my team come first; then comes the customer. I don't think you can really honor, respect, and dignify your people if you say that the customer is always right.*

Because there will inevitably be some passengers who'll misbehave and mistreat employees when you carry 100 million people a year, he gave me an example:

> *We had a lady who picked up a stanchion at a ticket counter and hit our customer service agent over the head with it. Am I supposed to say, "You're right. You're the customer."? No, you're wrong; we don't want to carry you again. You can't honor your own people if you say the customer is always right, no matter how much they abuse you. So, we don't tolerate abuse of our employees by our customers. And our employees love that.*

Virgin's Richard Branson agrees:

> *I think you motivate by genuinely caring about people,*
> *by putting your staff first, even ahead of the customer.*

Starbucks is also a company that puts its people first. CEO Howard Schultz believes that people and communities are fundamental:

> *We are in the business of people serving coffee,*
> *and not in the business of coffee serving people.*

He clearly understood the difference between these two concepts, which motivated him to make a habit of visiting 25 stores each week. Couldn't he have looked at the sales charts or indicators in the comfort of his office? Probably yes, but then again, he wasn't interested in numbers; he was interested in seeing as many of his people as possible. So, when Schultz returned to his CEO position after eight years in retirement, his first message to his people was: *"Starbucks is not—and never has been—about coffee. It's about you."*

None of these leaders refer to their people as "human resources." Instead, they refer to a "humanistic approach" and labor not only to "honor, respect, and dignify" each employee's "personal life," but to "genuinely care about" their "personalities," their "sorrows," "losses," and "joy."

Once you treat people as people, there are surprising consequences, not the least of which is the obvious profitability and success of the companies we've just mentioned. Although many of the executives that I've talked with throughout my professional career have told me that people are the most important factor in their businesses, they never speak of the idea with the same enthusiasm, frequency, or sincerity as Kelleher, Schultz, and Branson. And few of those executives are good leaders. Could it actually be that what separates truly stellar leaders from average ones has to do with being truly convinced that people are the most important part of your business, genuinely caring about them as people, and treating them in line with these values?

GREAT LEADERS DEEPLY AND GENUINELY CARE ABOUT AND TAKE CARE OF PEOPLE

By now I'm sure it's clear that leadership goes way beyond recognizing that you need people to achieve your goals, recruiting great teams, and managing talent. I think that what really sets great leaders apart from other bosses is that they genuinely and sincerely care about the people around them and take care of them.

Caring about the people is having attentiveness and the tendency to become aware of needs; taking care of people is assuming the responsibility and having the willingness to respond and satisfy needs. Although we've already seen aspects of both in what has come before in this chapter, let's explore these two aspects of caring in more detail.

Great Leaders Care About People

The traits of a leader? A person who really cares and loves the company and the people working in the company.
—Philip Kotler

*The important thing for somebody who is managing
people is that they genuinely care for people, that
they genuinely look for the best in people, that they
are good at bringing out the best in people.*
—**Richard Branson**

Yes, great leaders care about people, and when I say that they care about people, I'm not just talking about their work performance. What I mean is that they care about that person as a whole, as a professional, but also as an individual member of a family. They are concerned about what their coworkers are up to, what they're thinking, what they're going through, and what motivates them. These leaders don't see their teammates as "human resources" or "employees" (or in the case of a political leader, as "voters"). On the contrary, for these leaders, people are worth much more than a human resource.

Of course, each leader cares about her people in a different manner. In some leaders, this caring manifests itself as an extraordinary and extraordinarily sincere interest in those around them. In others, it shows in their desire to engage with people no matter where they are on the social or professional spectrum. In still others, it shows itself in the form of a belief in that person, genuine confidence that they can get the job done.

For instance, for more than five years I saw President Clinton at least a couple of times a year, when he participated in our events or when I took part in meetings of the Clinton Global Initiative. But the first time I met him was at Chicago's historic Arie Crown Theater, where he made an almost immediate, lasting impression on me. When he arrived for the event, we had to go to the greenroom through the private corridors and stairs normally used by the service personnel. At a junction between rooms, a server was holding a door, waiting for a colleague. With the president and his secret service escort, we went rushing past him. He stared at Clinton in deep admiration. When Clinton realized this, he stopped, turned around, and walked back a few steps. He shook the server's hand, said hello, and thanked him for his work. Though the gesture lasted for only a few seconds before Clinton continued on his original path, I am sure this man will always remember it and the sincerity with which it was conveyed.

Most executives say that people are the most important part of a business, but only a small percentage of those leaders actually practice what they preach. I still remember one occasion when a conference attendee approached me at the end of my lecture and said, "My boss always asks how I'm doing, but he never waits for my answer!"

Contrast this with President Clinton's behavior in Chicago. At that time, he had already completed his two terms in office and could not be reelected. He wasn't participating in any political campaign, so it was clear that he wasn't looking to gain anything in saying hello to the waiter. Rather, he chose to do so because he is innately dedicated to observing and considering people.

"The only other thing I think leaders have to do is understand not only policies, but people," Clinton said to me during our onstage interview in front of 2,000 executives a few minutes later. *"People ask me sometimes how did I become president coming from a small state that was poor, and I said I got to be president because I came from a small state that was poor."* What did he mean by that? What was his reasoning? Clinton continued:

My family didn't have a TV until I was 10. My parents' generation, my grandparents' generation never got any education, and they were brilliant. I grew up in

> *an environment where the guy that was pumping*
> *your gas could be as smart as the town doctor.*

He then revealed one of his keys to leadership:

> *So we were taught from early childhood to*
> *have an obsessive interest in people, to believe*
> *everybody had merit, everybody had a story*
> *and to imagine the impact of everything we said*
> *and did on someone else. That's what a leader*
> *needs to do, and the best leaders can do it and*
> *not be paralyzed by it, but be empowered by it.*

So, following Clinton's line of thinking, if some leaders deeply cared about people, if they were truly conscious of the enormous impact that they have on people, they "would be paralyzed." But great leaders feel empowered by it!

In any case, the key message here is "having an 'obsessive' interest in people," and it is this interest that comes across as and comes from true caring.

In all of our conversations throughout the years, Jack Welch always defined a leader as a "people person"—in other words, a person who is good at relating to people, at caring about people. When you're with Jack, even if it's just for 30 seconds, you get his full attention. He makes sure that, in that moment, you feel that you are the only thing that matters, and it is quite comforting to get such focused attention. I've seen dozens of people say hello to Jack, and in those few seconds of attention, like Clinton with the server, he was able to evoke both fascination and admiration.

Bill Conaty evoked something similar about his time with Welch:

> *I think that Jack and I hit it off. . . . We are both firm believers in people. We both come from humble beginnings, so you know, we don't have a problem relating to people right on the factory floor or to union leaders. What I loved about my job is that I was every bit as comfortable working with a union leader on the shop floor as I was with the CEO of the company. So it's that human aspect, it's that ability to really relate with human beings.*

Southwest's Kelleher also has a great interest in and adoration of people. When I asked him what his personal key to success had been, he said:

> *I've always been interested in people, and I've always liked people—all types of people, from all positions in life. And I enjoy formulating teams and getting people to cooperate in a worthwhile, hopefully inspiring endeavor.*

Herb was able to translate that same interest in people to Southwest's organizational culture and have a company that cares about them. It's no empty slogan that Southwest puts its employees first. That serious value comes straight from Kelleher and his interest in and care for all types of people. Think back to earlier, where he insisted that Southwest asks employees to be themselves, **"to have** *the liberty to be themselves at work."* He stated, *"We say: 'We didn't hire you because you're an automaton or a robot; we hired you because of your personality, so continue to be you at work.'"* In such a large company, this means a lot of different personalities to negotiate and make work together. Think back, as well, to Kelleher's insistence that, if someone at Southwest is in mourning or celebrating something, then the whole company is, too. Now, ask yourself, how would that even be possible if Kelleher and other managers at all levels were not interested in and did not promote a culture where people were interested in each other and concerned enough to know what was going on in their lives?

Leaders Give Considerate Feedback to Their Team

Another way of showing that you care about people is giving them constant and constructive feedback, particularly focused on positive commentary. By recognizing what someone is doing well, we create a powerful state of mind that encourages that person to continue growing, making an effort, and giving her best.

Welch once told me that he had more than 30 people that reported directly to him—something that seemed completely crazy to me—and that he would sit down on a regular basis with each one of them to follow up on their tasks and objectives. At the end of each meeting, he would write the person a small note explaining what he or she was doing well, and in which areas the person needed to improve. *"This took up approximately 60 percent of my time,"* Jack said, and I replied: "But how were you able to do that? When did you have time to do your job?" And he answered, *"But that was my job!"*

For Jack, each business review and miscellaneous meeting represented an opportunity to give feedback to his employees, and that was a crucial part of his management philosophy. Coaching teams is a task that leaders cannot delegate to anyone else, and it is possibly one of the most important roles they have in any organization. Leaders do not carry out many of the business tasks; rather, they delegate them. However, the tasks that a leader absolutely must perform himself are taking care of and following up with his team members.

Leaders Believe in Their People So That Their Team Can Believe in Them

Although it may seem trivial, getting to a point where you can say to a subordinate "I believe in you" is extremely powerful. If a leader is willing to bet on his people and really believes in every member of his team, not out of blind faith, but because he truly believes that they are the right people for the task, then they will also be able to say, "I believe in you" and follow their leader.

That's why I was so touched by the scene in *The Wolf of Wall Street* in which Jordan Belfort, the character played by Leonardo DiCaprio, asks one of his first employees if she remembers what she, as a single mom, asked him for when she started working there. She says that she remembers asking him for a check for $5,000 to pay for her kids' school and other debts. "So I gave you a check for $25,000," says Belfort, "because I believed in you!"

Isn't that great? Can you imagine the loyalty, self-esteem, and gratitude that this woman must have felt toward the person who believed in her that way? Moreover, this is an example of how the leader takes care of his people. Although Jordan Belfort may not be the ideal leader to emulate and the culture of Stratton Oakmont may not be one you'd care to pattern yours after, this curious incident demonstrates not only the way that belief and caring about people can grow and develop them—the woman stayed with his companies for years and became extremely successful in her own right—but also how taking care of your people can pay dividends to you and your organizational culture!

Great Leaders Take Care of People

> *And if the leader is successful in taking care of the followers—empowering the followers—the followers will take care of the leaders.*
> —Colin Powell

General Powell emphasizes that your followers have to believe in you. When they do, they'll follow your orders or general course because they will believe that you are guiding them in their best interest. You get them to believe in you by genuinely taking care of them, both from a professional and a personal point of view. He explains:

You get them to believe in you. You inspire them so they do what you want them to do because they think it is in their interest to do it. Then you make sure you take care of them. You give them what they need; you train them; you give them the tools; you give them the weapons, the equipment. You make sure they are well-fed, well-trained, well-housed—all their needs are taken care of. Only then will they believe in you.

It is important to note that belief here is a form of trust. If your people believe in you, then they will trust you; they will trust that what you're doing and asking them to do has a purpose that is also in their best interest and that, along the way, you will take care of them.

Jack Welch talks about fostering the "generosity gene." For Jack, it is the generosity gene that ultimately results in actions that benefit others—that is, your team. It means being genuinely interested in and developing a serious set of concerns around those employees, taking responsibility for their personal and professional growth and development, and making sure people are engaged, enjoying their work, and giving their best. In the end, it results in helping other people not only improve personally, but also improve financially and even become very rich! In his opinion, your care and dedication to people should be so intense that it becomes a part of your DNA. He insists that being a leader is not about you—it's about them, your people, and you should constantly attend to their development and well-being. He says it over and over again:

> *Don't ask what's in it for you or your company, but what's in it for them! Is it job security? Is it promotions? Is it personal growth? What is it? And communicate that to them.*

Unlike the challenge you have with a resource—which is how to use it effectively, efficiently, and productively, with the focus on the economic result for the shareholders—when you deeply recognize that employees are first of all human beings, the first concern you have is about them as people, as individuals in the quest for happiness, with their problems and their talents, with their passions and their fears. The outstanding results and productivity come as a consequence of taking care of your people *as people.*

EMOTIONAL IMPLICATIONS OF GENUINE CARING

Does everybody in this company feel as though they are a part of this? And if they don't, what can I do to achieve it? If I can capture every heart and every soul in this enterprise, I will have an outstanding company. That ought to be the objective!
—**Larry Bossidy,** CEO of Honeywell, 1991–1999

Throughout this chapter, we've touched on many things that bear on the emotional implications and impact of your relationship as leader with the people who make up your organization. As in the case of setting the vision, when you deeply and genuinely care about people and take care of them, you awaken a series of very powerful emotions and states of mind in your team members, and that has a tremendous impact on improving individual and team performance. As we conclude this chapter, I'd like to briefly take a more focused look at some of these emotions.

The first emotions that you instill when you care about and take care of the team you have created are *a sense of belonging* and *pride.* Saatchi and Saatchi's Roberts notes the importance of this to achieving results: *"I learned that a company that plays like a team and feels like a family operates at peak more often than other organizations."* The need to be part of a community is innately human, and a leader leverages that. Building a sense of belonging to a team is only the first of many concentric circles that a company must establish. The team, together with the rest of the employees, makes the company, and beyond that you have a whole ecosystem with distributors and customers. If you are able to create a solid, proud team, you can extend that power to the rest of the stakeholders in the business—in other words, create a sense of belonging for everyone involved in the community. An excellent example of this power is Apple, where each user and distributor is proud to belong to a circle that is changing the world through new technologies. Once a leader has created such a sense of community, he must make the people around him feel useful and important. He must make each member of the organization—internal *and* external—feel proud because they are an integral part of the company's success.

When you assemble the best team to pursue amazing dreams and achieve outstanding results, every single member of that team feels proud. Team members feel pride because they are aware of being part of something bigger than themselves, so you have to remind them about it! Furthermore, by discovering and recognizing team member talents, putting those talents to work, and ensuring that an employee does what she does best every day, a leader nurtures both individual pride and pride in the organization, as well as encouraging a sense of belonging by helping the person to see how she, her talents, her work, and her life fit into the vision of the organization. This is valuing each stone of the cathedral.

But there are more emotions to leverage when you care about and take care of people than just pride and a sense of belonging to the community. When you have everyone feel that they are a significant part of the team, they feel self-esteem, too. When you recognize the efforts, the improvement, and the results achieved by your people, when you show them that they are valuable on their own and for the project they are working on, you generate pride and self-esteem, yes, but also self-confidence and engagement. When you treat people as people, remind them that they can improve and learn from mistakes, believe in them, and show them the way, you foster this self-esteem and self-confidence. When all you do is geared toward helping every single person to develop and grow, when you show people that they have their own dreams, that they have to discover their own way of changing reality—therefore becoming leaders and not just followers—you give them a sense of purpose along with self-esteem and confidence. When you push people beyond their boundaries and comfort zones to get the best out of them, it creates pride and engagement in your team. (At the same time, it is such a treat, such a joy for you!) When you remind them of all the benefits they'll get by continuing with the planned work and achieving the desired results and when you constantly communicate how important the participation of each one of your team members is, you are generating true engagement and commitment to the community and to the cause. And, finally, being part of a team and a community, and genuinely caring for your people, creates *trust* that, as we shall see in Chapter 6, is one of the most important states of mind to facilitate collaboration at work.

The role of a leader is, therefore, to foster these numerous positive emotions through the specific actions and behaviors described. Being emotionally sensitive and intelligent is clearly an important and challenging endeavor. Consider, though, that over the course of this chapter we've talked about the relationship between a company's values, how its leaders treat their people, and the emotional implications of that treatment. Because values, in this sense, are at the heart of leadership, I would argue that ethics and leadership are interrelated. Because people are the center of business and one must care for and take care of them, leadership is, at heart, a moral and ethical enterprise—how one treats people or cares about them is a moral or ethical statement. This is an immense responsibility for a leader, but one must recognize and embrace it if one wants to be successful.

To check if you are leveraging this role of being all about people, I invite you to ask yourself the following question:

Do I genuinely care about the people who work in my organization, and do I do my utmost to take care of them?

CHAPTER 5

THIRD ROLE: COMMUNICATION

A leader must be someone who is able to communicate successfully.

—Jack Welch

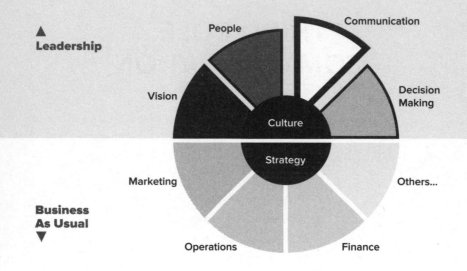

▲
Leadership

People

Communication

Vision

Decision
Making

Culture

Strategy

Marketing

Others...

**Business
As Usual**
▼

Operations

Finance

COMMUNICATION'S EMOTIONAL
IMPACT: CONNECTION AND TRUST

Jack's message is deceptively simple, but Tony Blair makes it clear that the stakes are high: *"If you cannot communicate properly, that's it, the game's over. . . . In today's world, you've got to be able to communicate . . . in clear and simple terms."* Herb Kelleher sums the issue up with clarity and a simplicity that belies the matter's import:

Communicate, communicate, communicate, and communicate.

Why does he repeat this word four times? Is once not enough? Does he also say, "Do the accounting, do the accounting, do the accounting, do the accounting"? He repeats the word *communicate* because the word alone is not enough to convey the significance of this idea and its importance to successful leadership.

Communication has two fundamental impacts. On the one hand, it conveys the information required to perform the activities included in the "business-as-usual" framework. Through appropriate communication you transmit objectives and provide the information necessary for every member of the organization to make appropriate decisions and complete her work efficiently. On the other hand, communication is a leadership tool that enables team building and allows for the creation of a true connection between group members; it builds the bond every group needs to perform at its best, because effective communication creates a positive state of mind through trust and the pride associated with a sense of belonging.

Although this chapter will certainly touch on the impact of communication on business-as-usual, I will mainly focus on the second impact, that of communication in its relation to leadership. This is because communication in terms of the Chief Emotions Officer's leadership has two critical aspects. First, it is key to helping a leader convey the terms of each of her roles. That is, it assures that everyone knows her vision, her concern for people, her organizational values and the consequent requisite behaviors, and her decision-making system. Second, communication builds a primary effect of its own: connection and the resulting trust. If you have been abundant in communication and consistent in what you think and feel, then and only then will you have created the necessary bonds and connections with your team to build trust, which is the ultimate goal and the emotion specific to communication.

The Three Levels of Communication

For you to be able to accomplish all of this, you will need to communicate effectively. In order, then, to ensure that everything you communicate has the greatest effect, you need to understand and mobilize the three levels of communication, each of which includes an outflow (something you convey to your peers) and an inflow (something you receive from them).

The first level of communication has to do with ideas and information. This dimension is closely related to the first impact, which is conveying the information required for day-to-day business processes. It includes all the talking and writing required to share ideas and information. It is the idea "outflow." In addition, it has to include the idea "inflow." Yes, it means that you also have to listen! Talking about your ideas and communicating them is just as important as listening to and considering others' ideas!

Leaders frequently forget about this, so we will return to it in more detail later.

The second level of communication refers to emotions—the inflow and outflow of emotions, which are what we call, respectively, to empathize and to inspire. "Inspiration" describes the outflow of emotions. My emotions are a source of inspiration. If I leave someone inspired, I have created an emotion in him. That is, I am an inspiring leader when I convey my emotions and my passion to my team and awake those same responses in them. "Empathy" is the inflow of emotions. When I am able to understand others' emotions, I am practicing empathy. In other words, if I am empathetic, I will be able to perceive the emotions that my team members are feeling. I feel inside what others are feeling. You can easily see how inspiration and empathy weave a sense of reciprocity. They bring me and my team closer together and are therefore an absolutely crucial "step" in the process of building bonds and ultimately establishing trust.

The third level of communication has to do with concrete behavior: what you actually do and what others in the team do, as well. In terms of outflow, it concerns acting and practicing what you preach, walking the talk, and delivering on your promises. People can very quickly tell when you keep or break your word. That is why it is also important to look people in the eye and use a type of body language that confirms what you are trying to express in words. Your body language and actions confirm or contradict what you say. Likewise, in terms of inflow, what other people are saying with their body language and their behavior is something that you need to be aware of and that you need to read, as these help you to understand the real motivations or intentions of others. The ultimate test for consistency between what people think, say, and feel is what they actually do and how they do it!

If I want to communicate effectively, I have to communicate on all three levels, both in the outflow and inflow of ideas and emotions, and by having everyone, including myself, walk the talk. In doing so, I will establish a genuine and deep connection with my people, which is an absolutely fundamental step to the ultimate goal of communication, building trust.

To put this in a different way, if you want to communicate effectively and reach the ultimate goal of establishing trust, you must first communicate all the business-as-usual information. Second, you must communicate everything concerning the other roles. Next, you inspire by communicating what you really feel and you are able to empathize with what your team really feels. You need to ensure that you do this in your actions and body language without fail. Then, and only then, through all of the above, will you be able to connect with your team and consequently build trust.

A Granular Model

Connection is why we are here. It's what gives purpose and meaning to our lives. What we know is that connection, the ability to feel connected, is—neurobiologically, that's how we're wired—it's why we're here.[1]

—**Brené Brown,** research professor at the University of Houston Graduate College of Social Work and author

Being a good person who knows how to listen and connect with people is absolutely a basic condition for a leader.

—**Carlos Ghosn,** chairman and CEO of Renault Nissan

When I think about communication having as a primary goal genuine connection that builds trust, I visualize the thousands of small daily exchanges that each person has with his or her sur-roundings. For the nature of communication is such that it occurs constantly, in every interaction.

Take a beautiful example from nature. Ants use a number of paths to go in and out of their anthills, and when one ant comes across another, they smell and touch each other with their anten-nas. Two ants never meet without some kind of communication. But what are they communicating to each other in these crucial moments of connection? Research indicates that these mini-meetings allow ants to find out, among other things, where the ants who went out in the morning found food, what kind of food they found, and what dangers they faced in the area.

We can easily apply this to our everyday life. On an individ-ual level, in order for me to make meetings and exchanges with my colleagues as meaningful and useful as they are for ants, it is necessary to be aware of all the aspects involved in daily meetings with my peers; these points of contact are opportunities to connect and contribute to building trust and conveying key information and emotions, which in turn makes people more efficient at work.

Moreover, communication is responsible for transmitting the DNA of the company's culture. As I mentioned before, commu-nication doesn't just concern the useful information applied to business-as-usual; it is also crucial for spreading passions, desires, and the pride that comes with belonging to a community. Com-munication connects each member of the corporate body so that they can trust each other and work toward the same vision.

Building Trust

In leading various companies over the years, one of the most valuable lessons I've learned is that establishing trust is the top priority. Whether you are taking over a small department, an entire division, a company, or even a Boy Scout troop, the first thing you must get is the trust of the members of that entity. When asked, most leaders will agree with this notion, but few do anything to act on it.[2]

—**Jim Dougherty,** senior lecturer at the
MIT Sloan School of Management

The final purpose of leadership is to inspire trust. This will lead to clarify the purpose. Then align systems, structures and processes to serve that purpose.

—**Stephen Covey**

Any communication has an emotional impact, provoking emotions from a sense of belonging to a sense of purpose and pride. But the most important emotion that you awaken when you enhance communication by utilizing the three levels discussed above—information, emotions, and action—is trust. To inspire trust should be an absolute priority of every leader, and she does that through the way she communicates.

Trust Is a Sign of Genuine Connection

Connection and trust are two aspects of the same phenomenon. Trust is the name we give to that emotion that is the result of making a connection. We are connected by a bond of trust.

Trust, then, is an incredibly important factor in putting together human groups and successfully navigating shared tasks. Sociologists and academics have written a great deal about trust, claiming that trust is an essential component of social capital because it makes cooperation easier. Trust predisposes our behavior to friendly attitudes and collaboration. If we trust each other, we will behave like friends, helping each other with our tasks to achieve our common goal.

This value is equally important in organizations. All companies have, by definition, multiple members that carry out different tasks. Organizations define different tasks and time frames for each member and articulate all these activities into a bigger goal, which is a product or service. But these tasks must be coordinated so that the final result can be achieved quickly and efficiently with the resources available. If these processes are well designed and all tasks are well defined, they theoretically lay the foundation for a solid company. Indeed, management is all about designing and defining these jobs with utmost precision and then making sure that all members strictly comply with the preestablished procedures.

Trust is the invisible but essential cement that allows an organization to coordinate countless tasks. Precisely defining and assigning tasks is not enough to have coordination and cooperation; you need people to trust each other enough to handle their job's interphase. People need to trust that if I ask you to do it, it will happen. Trust is that invisible connection that allows people to constantly fine-tune their work with the rest of the organization.

We've all seen how construction workers toss bricks from one person to the next, forming a chain that makes their work easier and decreases the physical intensity of the job. Ultimately, all tasks, all interactions between two people are just that; they are a way of tossing information around with the hope that the person on the other end is willing to catch it. That is trust: knowing that the next link in the chain will be someone who truly wants to catch whatever I'm producing or throwing his or her way, even if

I didn't toss it right! And that is why trust builds connection and enhances individual as well as team performance.

In preparation for a major event in Buenos Aires, I had the opportunity to have a long conversation with Manuel Contepomi, an incredibly successful rugby athlete who played on Los Pumas, the famous Argentine national team that came in third place at the 2007 Rugby World Cup. During our conversation, Contepomi told me about the importance of trust when making passes, and then he said: *"Well, Felipe and I are twins."* Intrigued by his response, I asked: "But what does your twin brother have to do with making or receiving a pass correctly or incorrectly?" Manuel explained that with each pass there's always the possibility of a slight delay that can be fatal for the person on the receiving end if, for instance, the opposing team is about to tackle the player. When playing with Felipe, Manuel had inherent trust, and it was the coach's ability to create a kind of trust among all the players similar to that experienced by twins that was, according to Contepomi, the key to making the Pumas a memorable team. He had participated in other teams where arguments, jealousy, and disputes kept the players from trusting each other, but the overwhelming trust on the Pumas team served as the invisible cement that integrated players' moves and dramatically increased the team's overall effectiveness. *"Leaders unleash astonishing potential by building trust,"* insists George Kohlrieser, psychologist, professor of leadership and organizational behavior, IMD, Switzerland, and bestselling author.

Now, do you think that this works differently in an office? Do you think that, without trust, employees can make proposals, suggestions, or requests, or actively participate in the search for new solutions and new ways of doing things? Can they complete tasks and increase productivity? No. Without trust, people wilt and hide behind their desks to work "by the book." Or worse!

Trust Enhances or Sabotages Performance

Building trust in an organization improves performance because it allows our brain to focus on the task at hand. Our brain constantly evaluates our surroundings to identify potential dangers. Generating trust means that I will avoid making constant decisions about certain people; I will simply assume that they don't represent any danger. Trust enables you to make decisions once and for all that the people around you don't represent a risk and that they will actually do things in your benefit, or at least toward a common goal. Such a situation then allows your brain to focus on a particular task. That is why trust enhances performance. If we don't have trust, we will constantly evaluate whether the actions of those around us represent a risk and consequently be distracted from our work goal.

Imagine the total absence of trust: paranoia. Could you imagine if all your coworkers were paranoiacs continually worried that everyone was plotting against them or that someone was going to stab them in the back? Imagine you are in a big meeting with 30 people to discuss a new business opportunity and you are convinced that 10 of those people are trying to kill you. Your brain will focus on every glimpse of a move made by any of the people in the room, jumping if they look suspicious. The focus is on survival, on identifying all possible sources of danger, and you then constantly make decisions as to whether a movement was to grab a weapon or scratch a back. Imagine the amount of energy such a state of mind would consume! Imagine how much more laborious it would make even the simplest tasks. Imagine what a drain on resources and morale it would be! Do you think, at the end of the meeting, you would have heard anything about the business opportunities? Of course not! Your brain doesn't have enough bandwidth. Trust is the invisible glue that is the result of and that stimulates fluid, candid, and effective communication with the rest of the team.

As Pat Lencioni, president of the management consulting company The Table Group, explained to me during a conference at Rockefeller Center in 2009:

> *What we really try to do is, first of all, make sure the executives have the capacity to trust each other because they understand one another and they have the capacity to argue with one another well. . . . But really with a big emphasis on trust. How can they trust each other and can they be vulnerable with one another. Can they admit when they are wrong, and ask for help? Humility, vulnerability and trust. . . . Without trust and conflict you can't possibly make decisions that people are going to commit to, and there is nothing to hold people accountable around.*

The vulnerability that accompanies trust is also the reason why treason is a capital offense and such a sin! I had clearly decided that you were a friend, and all of a sudden I got stabbed in the back. Consider the image! You only give your back in battle to your friends, because you trust them.

Now, in contrast to this environment of distrust and fear, think about the trust-building exercise regularly used in training sessions and retreats, where one employee must close her eyes and fall back, trusting that she will be caught by her coworker. Think about an office that runs on a sense of trust like that. Think about how easily the work would progress. You would have such a sense of trust in your colleagues, in their ability to perform their functions, in your relationship with them and your particular role in the organization, that the work would flow easily, almost as though without effort. An organization that runs on trust is much more efficient, not simply because its system of functions runs more effortlessly, but also because people are happy and confident.

FAVORING OPEN COMMUNICATION AND THE FREE FLOW OF IDEAS

It's about communication. It's about honesty. It's about treating people in the organization as deserving to know the facts. You don't try to give them half the story. You don't try to hide the story. You treat them as true equals, and you communicate and communicate and communicate.[3]
—**Lou Gerstner,** former CEO, IBM

One way to build trust and enhance performance is to foster open communication and not hinder the flow of information. An old adage says that whoever controls the information holds the power. Well, that's not the case anymore. Nowadays, information flows through thousands of channels, especially social networks, making it extremely difficult to control. Formal, controlled processes are only a small part of team communication. The business world we live in is further and further away from the seeming ideal of the past, where a few all-knowing engineers would define processes and authoritarian managers would control people to make sure they "did what they had to do." Information is no longer meant only for those in the highest ranks, but, rather, is distributed throughout the entire business structure.

A true leader must encourage a communication policy that promotes all three dimensions of successful communication between all members of the organization at every level. Communication does not just happen between me and my team or between management and employees; communication happens between everyone, all the time. If you are building trust, you can go directly up or down various organizational levels looking for the information you need, bypassing the chain of command. Bill Conaty says the following about his time at GE:

> *If you want a quick answer to a question and know that the person who can answer that question the fastest is three levels below you in the organization, as a manager, you have to go to that person and ask him the question and no one has to freak out about overstepping the chain of control and command.*
> *In our case . . . people got used to it and a way of communicating within the company that had not existed in the past because it had been suppressed by hierarchy.*

The Open Flow of Information Is a Goal

The open flow of information—unfiltered from the bottom up and the top down—is a true competitive advantage. Information puts everything in context, allowing different people in different parts of the organization to have a better understanding of what is going on, and consequently allows us to make better decisions. If we consider this, the ancient idea that "ignorance is bliss" and that it's better if I don't know what's going on around me "because it has nothing to do with my responsibilities" loses all rationale. The latter notion assumes that I am responsible for a strict set of tasks that was predefined by some enlightened person that somehow knew exactly what the company needed. However, this model is no longer realistic. We live in an era where changes occur quickly. The rate of change means that everyone has to be in touch with what's happening on the ground, as this ground is constantly shifting. We continually need new ways of programming and coordinating the tasks required to achieve results, so all employees must participate in a permanent process of adapting their tasks to new surroundings and to the rest of the company's operations. Moreover, we have to repeatedly interpret this reality, look into what clients want, and think about how to reformulate the value proposition itself. Services are not designed just once, but built every day. These responsibilities do not match any particular job description; everyone must participate in them. Contributions must be made by every person in the value chain. So, in order to constantly redesign processes, products, and services, leaders must encourage constant communication between all people involved in that process, giving each one a voice to constantly adjust the tasks—as in the case of construction workers tossing and catching bricks, always looking carefully at each other to fine-tune coordination.

Furthermore, if everyone is aware of what is going on in the organization, they will be less anxious and will be able to act with greater confidence. Being informed about what's going on in the rest of the organization will help you see the context in which each task is done and make it easier for people to focus on the task at hand. Ultimately, I insist, practicing open communication across the board creates deep connection and trust among all team members and frees the necessary flow of hard information so that every person can perform more efficiently and make better business decisions.

How, then, can we foster open and more informal communication among our team members?

Open Arenas of Informal Communication

A few ways to create more informal points of contact and more open communication of information and ideas are having comfortable cafeterias, multiple two-minute meetings at lunchtime, corporate universities, open-door policies, and even celebrations! Let's go over them quickly.

Company cafeterias are a great place to exchange informal information. Each person chooses to talk about whatever interests him, while others listen and engage or not. That is the biggest benefit of informal communication: there is no "big brother" deciding what each person can or cannot say, when each person should or should not listen. Steve Jobs knew this when he designed the office for Pixar from scratch and put the cafeterias and bathrooms in the center of the building to facilitate encounters. The conversations that occur in these spaces help build trust and connection.

Another executive who values cafeterias as arenas for communication is AB InBev CEO Carlos Brito. He eats lunch in the company cafeteria quite often so that he can have lots of informal "two-minute meetings"—a strategy that reminds me of the many mini-contacts that ants have with their peers when returning to the anthill.

Pixar University is another example of encouraging open, more informal communication. Pixar employees spend a certain number of hours per month in different classes at this company school, and they must take courses outside of their specialization. For example, an accountant can study the history of film or design, and a designer can take a class on psychology or cooking. This fulfills two major objectives: on the one hand, it trains workers in topics that are supposedly irrelevant to their responsibilities, but that provide them with a different context and a window onto the company as a whole, and, on the other hand, it allows distant members of the company, like accountants and designers, to talk and exchange ideas.

There are also even more extreme examples. Most organizations operate with a traditional model: sets of assistants, doors, and calendars to organize and manage what people have to say to each other. Other organizations, such as Tarjeta Naranja, the single largest non-bank credit card issuer in Argentina—and one of the most profitable—have *open-door* policies. Isn't that surprising? Since each person's opinion is equally respected, any employee can walk into any office at any time and express herself freely.

Furthermore, if "open" or "closed" CEO office doors have a huge impact on teams, imagine the repercussions of a CEO not having an office at all! Alejandro Char, former mayor of the city of Barranquilla, Colombia, went for months without entering his office. He walked around the city talking to people, and once he had identified a problem, he would call his team members and invite them to meet in a café or on the street to discuss a solution. Then there is Reed Hastings, CEO of Netflix, who seems to follow the recommendation of Tom Peters and Robert Waterman in their 1982 bestseller *In Search of Excellence* to do more MBWA or "management by walking around." He avoids having an office and spends his time in the midst of his people. Carlos Brito doesn't have an office either. Instead, he has a big room with a big table around which to hold conversations—and then there's the cafeteria!

Even something as seemingly simple as a celebration can be understood as an informal, open arena of communication. Far from being just a whimsy or a useless tangential activity, celebrating a company's milestones is actually an extremely important form of recognition. A celebration communicates achievement and praises the team for having done it together. When celebrating, you are saying, "We set out to do it and we did it as a team! Good for us!" You thereby foster the myriad positive emotions we've been talking about: sense of purpose, sense of belonging, trust, and pride. Celebrations are rich in emotional content and generate deep connections within the team, so don't overlook them!

FOSTERING COMMUNICATION: MULTIPLE DIMENSIONS

To be a leader you must communicate, and you can do it in multiple ways. . . . Am I communicating correctly? Yes, sure, because you are doing it from the heart.
—**Rudy Giuliani**

If communication is so crucial to creating connections between individuals, then we need to take some time to explore different modes of communication and why they are so effective in generating connections that produce results.

Communication is not a monthly newsletter from the personnel department; rather, it is everything that involves spreading information within the organization, as well as the emotional connections that are formed in the group. In light of this focus, the first thing we must do to achieve true communication is become aware of how we are communicating. As easy as it sounds, very few of the executives I know are aware of how they communicate.

On the Importance of Conversation

Perhaps the most obvious and effective means of communication is conversation. Conversations are a very important way of creating bonds. In fact, every conversation contributes to the formation of bonds. How? It's as Anselm Grün, a German Benedictine father, cellarer at Münsterschwarzach Abbey, counselor, and author, says, *"Every time I talk, I am only talking about myself."* Although you might think this is an overstatement, give it a second thought. Imagine you are in the middle of Times Square and you say, "These are amazing giant, colored billboards!" You might think you are just describing an element of reality, but reality is so rich that the element you choose to highlight actually reflects your own interests and the way you see the world. In the middle of Times Square, you could have said, "Wonderful architecture! I love the skyscrapers!" or "Interesting to walk and see people coming from all over the world and hear conversations in so many languages." or "How much would it cost me to put an ad of my product or service up there?" What you decided to communicate about gives me important information regarding who you are. Indeed, because whenever I talk, I only talk about myself, conversations are important means of transmitting who we are to each other. Through them, we get to know each other and are ultimately able to judge if we are friends or foes, if we can trust each other or not, and if we are working together toward a common goal or not. Through conversation, we try to establish trust, test the strength of bonds, and create connections.

The forms our conversations take are as numerous and contextually dependent as the kinds of bonds that we create through them. As a leader, you will need to be aware of not simply what kind of conversation is most appropriate for the circumstance, but also what type of conversation will be most effective in sparking the emotion that will achieve the result you want to attain at the end of the day. Therefore, let's take a moment to explore some different kinds of conversation.

Different Kinds of Conversations

Manfred Kets de Vries, distinguished clinical professor of leadership development and organizational change, INSEAD, asks if you have a culture where people can have creative conversations. Why? Because otherwise people don't learn. Indeed, the goal of *creative conversations* is to explore and learn. Most frequently recommended when a company needs to find new ways of seeing things, creative conversations generate novel ways of identifying problems or opportunities and addressing how to tackle them. As such, they are a crucial competitive advantage because they mobilize you to respond to change. Furthermore, creative conversations can act as a gauge of how much trust you've built because, in order to participate, team members cannot be afraid to speak up and offer ideas that might end up being discarded. As Carlos Brito says: *"[Trust] allows people to speak up in public without fear."*

This touches upon a critical characteristic of all successful conversation: *candor*, the quality of being open and honest. Candor means saying what you're thinking—the truth as you see it—in the clearest, most direct way possible. Some might say that it risks making people uncomfortable or causing conflicts, but I would argue that candor actually helps minimize conflict by exposing disagreements and encouraging that first step toward resolution. In fact, I believe that candor is one of the most effective ways to create trust. When I say things just as I see them, I'm being transparent; this allows me to build trust, which is, after all, the measure of belief in the honesty of another party. That's why candor is such an important element for leaders to exercise in conversation. If you build trust through candor, it will increase individual and group performance. Jack Welch's experience confirms this. When he was at the forefront of General Electric, one of the values he promoted as the foundation of all relationships in the company was candor, and we all know the success he had.

He once told me:

> *There's been a decline in the focus on leadership development, and I believe the reason is the damn computer. . . . Too many e-mails, too little face-to-face. You need more of those gritty conversations.*

In calling for more *gritty conversations*, Jack is of course implying the need for candor, particularly in the development of leaders, but he is also stressing the importance of face-to-face interaction in the trust conversations build. As we know, sitting behind a screen is quite different from sitting in front of people engaged in heated conversation. E-mails don't have the body language and emotional exchange that a face-to-face conversation has. We've all seen cases where e-mails create conflicts because the recipients misinterpret the general attitude or context of the written words—something that is much less likely in a face-to-face conversation. Beyond the possibility of greater misunderstanding, e-mails can undermine trust by what they allow people to hide. No one can see your reactions when you're just looking at your screen; moreover, you can easily edit them or omit them from what you send out. In contrast, when you're face-to-face with your coworkers, it's difficult to completely control your body language; plus, you often have no choice but to respond immediately and candidly—or risk building distrust by a hesitant and spluttering response. As a leader, don't shy away from the grit of a face-to-face interaction!

But what happens when candid, face-to-face conversations become a little bit too gritty? What happens when candor fails and communication is contaminated by conflicts between people?

As a leader, you have to be ready and able to handle or navigate *difficult conversations*.

Crucial Conversations author Joseph Grenny says that when we are in the middle of a complex or difficult conversation, we must do several things at once. First, we have to put our emotions aside. As we discussed earlier, they cloud our judgment and stop us from thinking clearly. So often, our emotions overtake us and compel us to focus on the thing that caused the emotional reaction instead of the actual issue at hand and a solution to it. Second, after putting emotions aside we must set the stage for collaboration by recognizing the other person's goals and indicating that we want to work toward a neutral, joint purpose. Finally, we should design a high-quality story that doesn't blame any external party. Stories of villains or victims are counterproductive. Instead of blaming, try to truly understand the other party and weave her needs into your story, thereby creating a new understanding and a collaborative outlook. It's worth it, as stories, which may seem childish and secondary to some, are actually crucial.

The Power of Stories

> *I think the best way to think about culture is that it is the mindset of the organization, how people think, that then drives the behaviors. And that mindset is in the form of a story—this is what cognitive science says. . . . [T]he leader needs to create a story and believe in that story.*
> —**Charles Jacobs,** author of *Management Rewired*

> *Stories are the single most powerful tool in a leader's toolkit.*
> —**Howard Gardner,** author of *Frames of Mind: The Theory of Multiple Intelligences*

The important role of stories in helping to resolve conflict sheds light on the overall power of stories as a mode of communication. In one of the most interesting interviews I've done to date, Robert McKee, author of *Story*, the Hollywood screenwriter's Bible, insisted on stories as the most effective form of communication. Why? Telling stories is the natural way for human beings to communicate, inherited from our ancestors. As humans, we are *"storytellers"* (and story listeners). Stories have played an important role in our development since the Stone Age because it is through stories that we have passed on information with the corresponding emotional content from one person to the next, from generation to generation.

This idea captures the two most powerful aspects of storytelling. First, it enables us to select and transmit data, facts, ideas, information, and messages. Second, it awakens and generates emotions. In storytelling, I not only communicate information, I also—or even mainly—convey and generate emotions. The audience listens first with the heart, then with the head!

This is why stories are a much more powerful form of influence than something like "reasoning," which McKee calls "the Power-Point" method of influence. Whereas the "PowerPoint" method relies upon rational argumentation and deduction—"Since a, b, and c mean this, the result is this"—stories contain both the rational and the irrational or emotional. Stories provide information, but, more important, they awaken positive emotions and generate empathy. As such, they offer a much more powerful impetus for people to perform and to get results. McKee concludes:

I have coached a number of IPO (Initial Public Offering) presentations to investors. When the entrepreneurs switched from inductive rhetoric to storified pitches, money flowed like water from a faucet.

It's the emotional side or effect of stories that seals the deal.

How does this work? Storytelling achieves the emotional transmission of information through its structure. In fact, it is the structure of stories that helps cause emotion. The structure of a classic story has a beginning, a development, and a resolution. The traditional beginning presents the main character and his objective or his "dramatic need": "Once upon a time, there was a man who . . . . Until one day . . . ." At this point the character starts out on a journey to resolve his problem or in search of his objective. During the development of the plot, we don't know if the person will reach his goal or not—if he will live or die, if his beloved will requite his love or not. We don't know until we arrive at the resolution.

Through such a story, the listener may learn crucial information regarding the dramatic event, but, much more importantly, she has the opportunity to identify with the main character and his struggles and to feel empathy toward him and his emotions. We identify with the character's desire to achieve his goals, the distress he feels when he is distanced from them, the joy he experiences when he wins small battles, and the final happiness or unhappiness.

Stories function similarly in a corporate setting, and in his book *The Seven Rules of Storytelling*, John Sadowsky[4] argues that storytelling is a powerful leadership tool. To begin with, stories allow you to formulate and communicate your purpose and goals, the vision and identity of the company, and examples of heroes and role model behavior. In fact, one of the most powerful tools we can use to create and sustain a community is storytelling. *"Stories weave teams together, and they give them a vision, a meaning, and a purpose. They don't just give them a sense of belonging, but one of possibility. Stories provide context and make people feel that they are part of a larger experience,"* explains Sadowsky. This means telling stories that explain how the community came to be and how it grew. Indeed, the most important thing you can do as a leader is to create a story that links your past and your identity with the future: "Once upon a time, a company dreamed of growing and becoming a leading business. . . ."

Gardner agrees: "Leadership involves the creation of powerful narratives, narratives that are much more than mission statements or messages. They are actually stories where there are goals and obstacles, where good and bad things can happen along the way and where the people involved feel part of an enterprise that's trying to end up in a better place."[5]

The second and arguably more important reason storytelling is so crucial to first-rate corporate leadership is that stories also generate the emotions required to subsequently fulfill the vision, purpose, and goals. By creating stories, you are not only able to convey the history of the organization, its culture, and the dream it has, but also to awaken the emotions people need to drive them to the ultimate goal. For example, a CEO might use the main character in a story of trial and hardship to inspire team members to identify and empathize with the role models who made the organization great and thereby push through a difficult time or achieve higher numbers. Or he might narrate the dangers the company faced in the past to rally employees in the present: "When our company was very small and barely getting by, large competitors were always attacking us, but we managed to survive thanks to the heroic hard work of our employees." This is similar to how companies like Apple or Virgin, when they were in their early stages, chose to pit themselves against their large competitors, Microsoft and British Airways, to create stories of a drive for survival against a larger foe—like David and Goliath.

These sorts of stories clearly have a strong pull on human beings, so use the power of your story! Identify your company story's epic value; seek out anecdotes that represent your values.

Use foundational moments to convey a sense of belonging and the road to success. As we discussed earlier, by giving your people a sense of purpose and belonging, by fostering trust and bonding, you will enhance individual and group performance. Stories are a prime tool for doing this!

LISTEN UP: A FEW NOTES ON LISTENING AND ITS BENEFITS

In this section we've seen different ways of fostering communication, from various forms of conversations to open arenas and celebrations. I have explained why all those activities not only increase the sharing of data, information, and ideas—very useful for the business-as-usual activities in today's fast-changing world—but also and above all create multiple opportunities for everyone in an organization to connect with each other, facilitating and enhancing the building of trust and the resulting bonds among team members.

That is why communication is a powerful leadership tool—because ultimately it creates trust, and trust is essential to collaboration and increasing individual and group performance. In conclusion, though, I think that it is crucial to highlight an aspect of conversation and communication that we have not yet explicitly addressed, despite the fact that it underlies the success of every type of communication we've concentrated on in this chapter. The key to having fruitful conversations—and therefore effective communication—is listening! Listening is the critical aspect that goes hand in hand with articulating your ideas and generating the inflow that closes the loop of conversations. What you have to communicate is not the only important thing; what others have to communicate is equally important. In fact, the most effective thing a leader can do is to listen to his people, because listening and understanding inform all forms of communication—whether it's gritty conversations, celebrations, or storytelling.

We can explore the value of listening across many dimensions. First, listening allows you to access relevant information, both on specific topics and, more specially, on those things related to the minds and hearts of your people. It allows you to understand who the other person is, what she thinks, and what she feels. Listening enables you to identify the concerns, as well as the sources of satisfaction, in each of your team members. When the leader asks questions, listens to his team's answers, and considers all those responses and points of view, he is taking advantage of the information exchanged and more.

Additionally, he is encouraging constant learning and showing that he is willing to have his opinions transformed. Colin Powell has told me two anecdotes that demonstrate this. He said he had a telephone line that not even his private secretary was allowed to answer. Only about 10 people had that number, people he trusted to call and tell him what no one else around him would say: "Last night on TV, you were completely wrong in what you said" or "I think what you are doing is a big mistake and my neighbor agrees with me." He also surrounds himself with people he expects:

to challenge me, to argue with me. This goes down to the most junior people. . . . I had captains coming to brief me, and I would challenge them to argue with me. I needed captains that would say to me, "No, general, you are wrong. This is the right answer." And he is supposed to have the right answer because that is [his] specialty. I want people that don't hold back information.

Powell clearly values the role of listening in the constant learning necessary to be a good leader.

That doesn't mean that you will always do as people ask or suggest. As we shall see in the next chapter, a leader must make her own decisions. But acting unilaterally, without even listening in the first place, does not have the same effect as being empathetic and taking the time to listen to people—even if afterward you say: "I understand your point and I respect it, but I'm convinced we have to do something else" and act according to your own convictions. When people feel that someone was listening to their opinions, they are then more likely to support the final decision, even if it doesn't coincide with their own judgment.

Listening is rare and, therefore, extremely powerful! It is the foundation of genuine communication and, therefore, helps develop connection and trust. For a leader, it informs all modes of communication, and communication is a primary role in the strong, effective leadership that characterizes the Chief Emotions Officer.

To check if you are leveraging the role of enhancing communication, I invite you to ask yourself the following questions:

Are you connected with your people?
Do you generate trust?

CHAPTER 6

FOURTH ROLE:
DECISION MAKING

*My work as president could best be described
as Chief Decision-Making Officer.*
—Bill Clinton

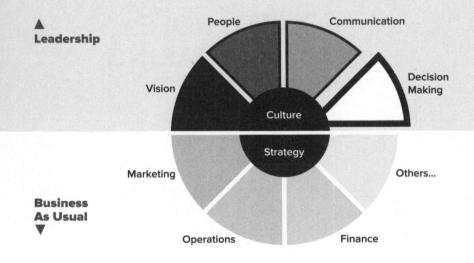

Leadership ▲

People

Communication

Decision Making

Vision

Culture

Strategy

Business
As Usual
▼

Marketing

Others...

Operations

Finance

I was surprised by President Clinton's words. Why would one of the most outstanding leaders in the world describe decision making as his main role when this topic is missing from almost all existing literature on leadership?[1] For instance, neither the 2011 *HBR's 10 Must Reads on Leadership* nor Frances Hesselbein and Alan Shrader's two-volume compendium *Leader to Leader: Enduring Insights on Leadership* (1999 and 2008) contain articles whose explicit focus is decision making. This lack of emphasis in leadership literature on decision making is paradoxical because many great leaders, like Clinton, see their ability to make decisions as a fundamental tool through which they fulfill their role. They make decisions about how to direct resources and efforts toward their goals, while simultaneously benefiting team members, encouraging their commitment to the goal, and making them feel like they belong.

Although the existing academic literature on the subject focuses on decision making as it relates to "information," in this chapter I do not intend to address "operations research" or any other information management science. Rather, I will try to highlight the various dimensions of decision making under the control of the leader and the far-reaching impact that these aspects have on each team member and the group as a whole.

If we consider the different aspects involved in decision making, the most relevant for a leader tend to be:

- Managing information (hard and soft, conscious)

- Creating a strong decision-making system

- Managing emotions in decision making

- Managing unconscious information: intuition and judgment

- Making *your* decision

I will not touch on the first point regarding hard information or techniques for managing it; these are more relevant to information management science than to our current focus. Instead, I will focus on the other four factors, as they are the ones that help us to understand the relation between emotion, culture, and decision making so vital to the successful leadership of the Chief Emotions Officer.

THE FUNDAMENTALS OF A STRONG DECISION-MAKING SYSTEM

Decision making is intimately linked to execution because in business the process of deciding and ordering a series of tasks must be monitored until the final action is carried out and the goal met. Therefore, the first step on the road to the successful execution of a task is to set out the criteria we will use as guides to pursue the priorities and objectives; these criteria are the dimensions that allow decisions to be made along the way.

Defining the Decision-Making Criteria

Once a set of priorities is established, the posterities become implicit. Logically speaking, this means that when I choose which criteria are to be applied first, I am also defining which are to be applied last. This is where the *values* and *strategic behaviors* of a corporate culture become so important.

An organization identifies and promotes certain values and strategic behaviors as part of its decision-making criteria. That is, values and strategic behaviors are common criteria for decision making in any company. In fact, if we take a closer look, a company's sets of values and strategic behaviors *create* a system of decision-making criteria. The values and behaviors you foster in the organization are absolutely fundamental because of their influence on the thousands of small decisions that are taken in every organization daily. As a matter of fact, you get a good picture of how employees across the organization will make decisions if you look at the values and desired strategic behaviors of the company. Employees are faced with thousands of dilemmas and choices at work every day, and they will end up making decisions based on those values and behaviors. If, as a leader, you have clearly identified these values and behaviors, everyone in your organization will make decisions in accordance with them, even when they are making decisions based on more specific criteria.

In order to better understand the critical role of values and strategic behaviors in guiding decision-making criteria, we need to remember the distinction I made between these two concepts earlier in Chapter 4. I use the term *values* when it relates to how I perceive people, where they are on my priority list, and how I treat them, whereas I use *behaviors* when it is more business-related. In short, a value refers to people and their relationships, whereas behaviors are related to the actual implementation of a value in a business setting. In both cases, they are the two ends of the decision-making system. A "value" is something you give importance to, and it becomes a "behavior" through a decision. For example, as we said earlier, if "honesty" is a value, each time I am confronted with the possibility of a bribe or any other dishonest choice, I will make a decision to behave in the right way.

We can see an example of the distinction between values and strategic behaviors and its relation to decision-making in the "Family Core Values" of Zappos.com.[2] If I separate Zappos's 10 key points into values and strategic behaviors, as I defined them above, it looks like this:

Values:

1. Create fun and a little weirdness.

2. Be adventurous, creative, and open-minded.

3. Pursue growth and learning.

4. Build open and honest relationships with communication.

5. Build a positive team and family spirit.

6. Be passionate and determined.

7. Be humble.

Strategic behaviors:

8. Deliver WOW through service.

9. Embrace and drive change.

10. Do more with less.

The list of values does not give us a clue as to what kind of business Zappos is in. Rather, it demonstrates the values Zappos seeks when hiring and how it expects the people it would decide to take on as a part of its team to comport themselves. For example, the attitude Zappos people have to have toward change is one of "open-mindedness," "learning," and "adventure." These values reflect Zappos's need as a company in a particular market to pay close attention to the reality of situations as they develop and to learn to adapt to them. Moreover, this list of values is an "operational guide" to help employees make daily decisions regarding their job and how to get along with their colleagues. As for the relationships between colleagues and employees, it is very specific: Zappos expects everyone to be "open" and "honest" and to build a team and "family" spirit! Therefore, whereas other companies might just value "professionalism" or "excellence," showing that knowledge and results are more valued than building long-lasting bonds, Zappos's values forefront the importance of its people and make clear that certain cutthroat behaviors wouldn't be tolerated. This, in turn, stems from Zappos's general attitude toward life and challenges, and that is "fun," "determination," and "passion." It thus creates a working environment very different from one that only values just "respect" and "excellence." Through these values you can see that the decision-making criteria that drive Zappos come from a humanistic point of view.

Now consider the short list of behaviors manifesting the company's values. This list makes complete sense when looked at through the lens of Zappos.com and its strategy. Online shoe sales is a very low-margin business that has traditionally been focused on costs. To avoid this situation, Tony Hsieh purposefully decided to differentiate his business based on amazing service. For example, if a person buys a product at 6 p.m. in New York, and Zappos .com is committed to delivering the product within 48 hours, an employee at the company might decide to put the product on a plane from Zappos's Kentucky warehouses that same night so that the customer has the product on her doorstep the next morning. What a wonderful surprise that would be! The customer can also order up to 10 pairs of shoes to try at home. Once the customer has picked which pair she likes, she sends the others back to Zappos—with all shipping costs paid by the company!

In both of these examples, the criterion that employees use to guide their interactions with customers is "Deliver WOW through service." When you have that behavior explicitly in the mind of every employee and the situation comes—say on a Monday night at 10 p.m., when the employee is on his own and needs to make a decision whether to save a few dollars or surprise the customer— you know which criterion he will use to make the decision.

Any of these proposals could be copied by the company's competitors at a moment's notice, but in order to stay one step ahead, Zappos invites its employees to "embrace and drive change." Can you imagine, working in a company like this, saying to your boss: "We can't change this because we've always done it this way and it works"? Of course not! That's why all companies must choose appropriate values and strategic behaviors so that they will be in line with the business's objectives.

We can also consider Kelleher's Southwest Airlines in terms of clearly defined decision-making criteria based on values and behaviors. The customer service department's flexibility and initiative is crucial to perfectly executing the company's culture, so, when Herb once saw a sales representative flipping through a 500-page manual to figure how to treat a customer, he realized that something was not working. Decisions regarding customer service cannot be executed via a manual as though they were the results of a computer program. Herb wanted to trust his employees to be able to make decisions based on the company's vision, values, and behaviors: stellar customer service provided by empowered employees. He ended up burning all of the manuals. He elaborates on this in the following way:

We now have only general guidelines. If we lean toward the client, giving a good service, then it's OK. If an employee makes a decision that benefits the client but ends up being costly, we reward him but ask him not to do it again. I remember that once, because of the bad weather, we couldn't fly from Baltimore to Long Island. An employee that had only a few months in the organization hired four buses to take the passengers to their final destination. We rewarded her for her initiative!

When employees know what is expected from them in terms of values and behaviors, they don't lose time deciding how to behave in a given situation. That's what happens when criteria are clear—when the culture is clear and strong. When the culture is weak and the decision-making criteria are unclear or ill-defined, employees waste their time trying to guess what they have to do and how to do it, and they have a much greater probability of making the wrong or even detrimental decision.

By appealing to values and strategic behaviors, we can establish general decision-making criteria and ultimately the way in which the organization intends to implement those decisions. When CEOs clearly state values and behaviors, it is as if every team member had a small boss in his head making decisions as if they were made by the CEO herself. They will make decisions, as Carlos Brito, CEO of Anheuser-Busch InBev, puts it, *"as if he or she were the owner."*

As you certainly know, underlying the values and behaviors of an organization is its vision or dream, so when considering decision-making criteria, we can't stress enough how important vision is in giving and guiding important decision-making criteria. If people in the organization are clear about the company's vision and strategy, they work toward it with each decision. These decisions are not about optimization, doing things a little bit better, but rather fulfilling our purpose, getting closer to our desired dream. Indeed, it is essential that all members know where the company is going so that the dozens of decisions that each employee must make on a daily basis are governed by the company's vision and strategy and its desired values and behaviors. In one of our meetings, Kelleher told me that an external consultant had conducted a survey of the airline's staff and was surprised by the results. "This is incredible, regarding the company's vision and strategy, 80 percent of the people gave the same answers as you!" said the man in charge of the survey, to which Herb replied with a big, knowing smile. In Herb's opinion, the survey results represented a victory for his corporate culture and an affirmation that strategy and vision are effective guides of behavior only when everyone is on the same page about them.

Establishing a Decision-Making System

> *The first and most important principle for me is that good decisions are based upon good decision-making processes. . . . [T]o make a sound decision, you have to engage in a decision-making process that is disciplined and rigorous.*
> —**Carly Fiorina**

> *CEOs have to make key decisions. Of course they do, but in general what they have to do is stimulate a process in which other people are taking effective decisions. That means that what they really do, what I believe is more important, is create a system, a structure, a philosophy, or a culture that allows people to make the right decision.*
> —**Henry Mintzberg**

Making decisions doesn't mean simply "thinking" or "saying" that I'm going to do something, or that one choice is better than another. When I talk about decision making, I'm referring to a *system*, a whole set of actions triggered by inner determination, which then extends to designating who will execute that decision and the human and/or material resources necessary to do so. In fact, one might argue that this decision-making system is a funda-mental structure in that it *includes everything*: the decision-making criteria, who makes the decision, the delegation process, the emotional management, the controls, the rewards, and so on.

Whether or not she is fully aware of it, once a leader understands the criteria guiding decisions, she must create a decision-making system that gives shape to how her employees will execute the criteria. It is this system that permits colleagues to use the criteria as a guide for how to pursue the priorities and objectives. Moreover, as assigning clear responsibilities is crucial to successful execution, defining a good decision-making system is the first step to implementing a delegation process. To determine who decides what, the decision-making system must include a number of levels in which independent decisions may be made, plus a list of circumstances under which the decision will be escalated—for example, decisions regarding how much money to invest, or sensitive matters such as hiring and firing personnel. It is typical and desirable that staff at each level, starting with the entry-level employee, have a scope of decisions that they can make according to predefined criteria. Take, for example, amount of investment. If that investment threshold is achieved, then the decision is taken by the next level, and so on.

Creating a Delegation Process

Delegation is a crucial part of the decision-making system. Since a leader can't possibly make all the decisions facing a company, she has to transfer some decisions to others and allow other people to participate in the process to the best of their abilities.

The challenge is to delegate properly. Here, I'm going to focus on the features of delegation that have the largest impact on our role as leaders, and though it may seem surprising, I will try to show how handling delegation in a certain way ultimately helps develop the self-esteem and sense of trust that the people who work for you feel—and, as a result, helps produce a culture of greater success. The five fundamental factors of delegation are:

- Who decides what? Choose whom you delegate to and provide them with clear objectives, criteria, and resources so that they can make and implement decisions.

- Support that person in his or her decisions, both the good and the bad ones.

- Take responsibility for your decisions and learn from your mistakes.

- Build team members' self-esteem and confidence.

- For tough decisions, intervene in the process and take charge.

Who Decides What?

As a first step in the delegation process, a leader needs to ask herself a deceptively simple question: "Who decides what?" I say "deceptively simple" because this question contains in a nutshell two considerably more complex questions: "What needs to be decided?" and "Who are the most appropriate people to delegate those decisions to?" In answering these questions, you are actually creating a "mini decision-making system." That is, you are identifying the objective and specifying what all the elements involved in decisions around it are, as well as naming the subordinate who will be responsible for them.

First and foremost, then, delegating means clearly defining the objectives, criteria, and resources necessary for others to make and implement decisions. That's the "what." Then there's the question of who makes a decision. When I think about leadership and decision making, I naturally focus on those decisions that, given their huge impact, are vital to the organization and, thus, fall upon the leader. However, these may only be 10 percent of all decisions made. So it is key to consider the other 90 percent of decisions that are delegated to other team members—the result of the decision-making system the leader has put in place. Both are clearly crucial to an institution, so in order to successfully delegate, a leader must identify the most appropriate person to assume the remaining responsibilities—the person most capable of executing the delegated tasks and decisions. To do that, it is crucial that the leader identify key points, such as where information comes from, who has the specific knowledge and experience necessary to make decisions, and how to ensure that action is taken at the right level. Once this has been accomplished, a leader should assign clear responsibilities.

Let me illustrate this with a couple of examples. Imagine an HMO faced with a patient with a complex medical situation who is asking for certain coverage and very specific medical service providers. Who better than the medical director of the HMO to decide what to do, particularly if he has very clearly in mind what the company's purpose, values, and behaviors are? You need to trust the person who knows each topic; you need to delegate with clear criteria to the one who knows best.

Similarly, imagine there is a situation in a hotel restaurant. The waiter brings the dishes to the table, and one of the guests doesn't receive the fish she ordered, but, rather, some pasta. The waiting time has already been longer than they had all expected, so the guests are clearly upset. The waiter realizes they are right and has to make a decision on the spot as to how to deal with the situation. He immediately says: "I sincerely apologize, madam. The wine you are all drinking is on me, and I'll have the chef immediately prepare the fish for you." Instead of calling the manager and explaining the situation to him, the server, who had all the knowledge of the problem, handled the situation himself. That is why some hotels, in addition to having well-defined procedures, allow each waiter or front office clerk to decide to break those procedures and spend up to a certain amount without asking any supervisor for permission. These workers are close to the problem at hand; they know the values and strategic behaviors they should observe and the general criteria the company has; they are, therefore, in the best position to decide—of course, all the while remaining accountable for the decision taken. Most decisions in a company are made by people like the medical director or the waiter. That's the day-to-day operation and why delegation and to whom one delegates are so important.

Support Team Members in Their Decisions

Once we have defined the decisions to be made and identified who should make each of them, a critical aspect of team building is always to support the person in each decision he makes. It's not about simply making him feel more confident in comfortable, low-risk positions, but about backing him up in the face of the bosses, vendors, or customers. Decision making is about trade-offs, so even right decisions generally have a cost or downside to them. Backing up an employee is not easy when there is a cost associated with a right decision; it is definitely difficult when the decision is the wrong one. Supporting your people means taking responsibility for the costs whether or not the decision leads to the desired results. If a member of my team makes a mistake while making a decision within the framework of his responsibilities— and within the framework of legal and ethical behaviors—I have to support him. This doesn't mean that I shouldn't correct the error or modify the decision, but I must always support the person who made it.

We are all afraid of making decisions because of the consequences of making the wrong choices, so when a leader takes the burden of backing up his staff on his shoulders, he relieves the team member of that same burden. It requires courage on the part of the leader, but it shows commitment to the individuals in the organization and the will to build a strong, close team. By backing up your people, you help them grow; you increase their confidence and self-esteem. Moreover, you create a team spirit and a sense of belonging.

Take Responsibility for Your Decisions, Learn from Your Mistakes, and Be Flexible

> *When I have to make a decision, I always ask myself what are the consequences if I am wrong.*
> —**Alan Greenspan,** chairman of the
> U.S. Federal Reserve, 1987–2006

Obviously, the support is unconditional and totally mandatory when your team members have made a decision at your request or according to your instructions.

Former Colombian president Álvaro Uribe Vélez provides us with an exceptional example of taking responsibility for the consequences of a decision executed by his team that he made as a leader. At the end of February 2008, President Uribe was notified where the terrorist Raúl Reyes, one of the top guerrilla commanders in the country, was supposedly hiding out. Although the terrorist's location was very close to the Colombian border, the coordinates indicated that he was actually in Ecuador. Uribe had to decide whether or not to order an air strike. He finally ordered the bombing. The military attack was successful in killing Reyes. However, it also caused a serious diplomatic problem with Colombia's neighboring country because it violated sovereign borders without having attained the Ecuadorian government's permission in advance.

Many of his advisors, as well as diplomatic "best practices," indicated that if Uribe handed over the head of the air force and made him responsible for the raid, he could lower tensions between the two countries, but the president flatly refused. *"Never!"* said Uribe in an interview with me. *"I couldn't do that, because I was the one who gave the order."* This type of behavior, where a leader takes clear responsibility for his team acting on his decision, is much more than a specific strategy—it is a deep and fundamental part of building credibility and loyalty within your team. In the case of Uribe, it built an amazing loyalty from the armed forces.

Uribe's actions demonstrate the fundamental need for the decision maker to take responsibility for the consequences of a decision. Indeed, as a leader, once a decision has been implemented, you must hold the person who made the decision accountable for it, even and especially when that person is you.

This includes, in particular, the costs and aftereffects of mistakes. Says the former president of the Colombian people: *"Leaders should take responsibility for failures."* At the same time, a leader should share successes resulting from his decisions with others. Indeed, a good leader is confident enough to share the credit when things go well and accept the full weight of failure when things go wrong. President Uribe did just that whenever it came time to share news: when the news was good, his ministers were responsible for communicating it, thus enabling them to share in the recognition and get the credit they deserved. When the news was bad, Uribe communicated it himself, taking the responsibility squarely on his shoulders.

After assuming responsibility, you must learn from the results of the decision, good or bad. Of course, this process is much easier when the decision is correct the first time around, but it is much more important to identify and learn from failures. After all, errors and mistakes are an inherent part of all human activity and decision-making processes. Steve Jobs knew this. He once said: "Some mistakes will be made along the way. That's good because at least some decisions are being made along the way. And we'll find the mistakes and we'll fix them. And I think what we need to do is to support that team."[3] Only by systematically reviewing the team member's decision will a leader be able to guarantee that everyone will learn and grow from the process. Nothing hinders innovation more than an organization that is afraid of mistakes and that punishes people for making them. Instead, one should support people and encourage them to actively learn from mistakes.

Learning, however, is not simply learning after a decision has been made and you have seen the results or consequences. It also means being open to change midway through the decision-making process. A leader often has to correct or change his decision midcourse. As Colin Powell insists,

> *You must not hang onto your ego or your past success. Be passionate about what you think, but not so in love with your original idea that you ignore when it's time to change it. If you want to be successful, you have to be ready to throw that which is no longer relevant overboard.*

Powell experienced this situation firsthand when the Soviet Union was dissolved in 1991. At that moment, everything he had prepared for throughout his long and celebrated career—the Soviet threat—ceased to exist, a situation that Soviet leader Mikhail Gorbachev summed up in one sentence: "General Powell, you're going to have to find another enemy!" Faced with this rather atypical situation, Powell was forced into a difficult decision: to reduce the armed forces by one million members. He also had to make critical decisions about reducing the number of suppliers to the U.S. Army, which meant that, in order to survive, they had to change their business models and often merge with other companies. *"You must not hang onto your past success,"* repeats General Powell, because if you do, you won't be able to make the right decisions and change in time.

We see, then, that in order to create a successful decision-making culture, one must make sure people take responsibility for their decisions, but one must not punish them; instead, one should support them and encourage them to actively learn from mistakes. That includes the leaders themselves; they have to set aside their egos to learn and to adjust their decisions to the fast pace and ever-changing series of circumstances business throws at them. Only by doing so can a leader ensure that his decision-making system will not simply enable the organization to survive, but actually also build the self-esteem and foster the growth necessary to create success.

Build Team Members' Self-Esteem and Confidence

Tomorrow's leaders will have to be incredibly sure
of themselves and be very emotionally stable.
—Carlos Ghosn

Ghosn also insists that effective delegating—which includes learning after making the decision—strengthens each person's leadership skills and distributes leadership throughout the entire organization, both horizontally and vertically.

Indeed, by delegating, allowing people to make their own decisions within a clear framework, and supporting them as they take responsibility for and learn from the consequences of those decisions, you help them grow as people and as leaders themselves. You help them grow professionally and personally by building their self-confidence and self-esteem through the decision-making process. When people have higher self-esteem and confidence, they work better, individually and in groups, so growing these emotions in your team should be a priority for any leader.

Sam Walton, the founder of Walmart, once said: "Outstanding leaders go out of their way to boost the self-esteem of their personnel. If people believe in themselves, it's amazing what they can accomplish."[4] That's right—if people believe in themselves, it's amazing what they can do! But backing your team not only builds confidence and self-esteem; it also provides them with the emotional support that favors learning.

I am sure that this process is psychologically similar to what I do as a father as my children grow: when they are young, I give them a scope for making small decisions, which then transition into more important ones, and I provide them with the certainty, affection, and confidence they need so that they'll know that I am there to help them take responsibility for any consequences. This trial-and-error process, and the parental support that goes hand in hand with it, increases the child's self-esteem and builds his confidence. As the Chief Emotions Officer, I should follow the same procedure. The key to achieving this is a process of delegation, accountability, learning, and, above all, confidence in people.

In contrast, think about what happens under opposite conditions: when a person's self-esteemed is destroyed, you only get worse results. Concentrating decision making in the hands of a few or arbitrarily interfering in a subordinate's decision for no reason destroys the team and undermines confidence. A manager or employee who has no self-confidence not only makes the dumbest mistakes, but ends up a broken person. The amazing thing is that when the same person changes departments or gets a new boss, he suddenly recovers, thanks to this new mentor, his self-esteem and good performance. Think back to the example of the marketing analyst I gave in Chapter 2!

By delegating and both backing and trusting my employees' judgment based on the values and strategic behaviors of corporate culture, I'm working to consolidate a group of people trained to make important decisions and continue growing, professionally and personally.

For Tough Decisions, Intervene in the Process and Take Charge

> *A leadership skill—in a world of uncertainty—is the ability to make tough decisions. That takes courage.*
> —**Paul Schoemaker,** coauthor of *Winning Decisions: Getting It Right the First Time*

However, on certain occasions the leader must intervene in the established decision-making process and go around it in order to make a particular decision. When the "potatoes are hot" and nobody wants to "grab the hot potato," a leader steps in and makes the decision. For instance, at the height of the Mexican peso crisis in 1994–1995, President Clinton decided to back Mexico, as he told me, *"in spite of my advisors"* and in the face of immense opposition in Congress. Even with a decision-making process in place, at some point all great leaders must disregard that system and make their own decisions, following their gut feeling, intuition, or judgment. This happens when there is no "correct" or "ideal" decision to be made, as much as the group may strive to find one. In those moments, the leader must make the decision he believes to be the best option—his *own* decision—and align the team behind it. We will explore this more specifically later when we discuss making *your* decision and crisis management.

Even when a leader must intervene in the process and make a tough decision, he will need to be aware of the emotional effects and consequences this will have and, as we have explained, take responsibility for them at the same time as he also safeguards his employees' self-esteem, confidence, and ability to develop as leaders in their own rights. As you can see here, the decision-making role of a leader has as much to do with being responsible for the emotions of your team—including your own—as it does with the hard variables of a decision.

MANAGING EMOTIONS IN DECISION MAKING

Decisions are not risk-benefit; they are not a computer. [The process] cannot lack emotions, which are the engine on which it runs.
—Álvaro Uribe Vélez

It goes without saying that, if building emotional states like self-esteem and confidence is such an important aspect of a leader's decision-making role, then managing those emotions goes hand in hand with managing his own. In the coming section, we will explore the role emotion has in a decision, the emotional impact a decision has on the team, and the need to manage emotions that arise from both of these.

Before we delve into managing emotion, it's important to understand a bit more about the place of emotion in decision making. Emotions play an important, undeniable role in decision making, both for the leader and for the individual members of a team. Recent research has demonstrated that emotion is a crucial part of people's planning and decision-making process, and that the difference between emotion and reason is not as clear as we used to think it was. In fact, people like Saatchi & Saatchi CEO Kevin Roberts insist that 80 percent of consumer decisions are emotional, not rational. People may think they make the decision in a logical manner, but those decisions are actually the product of emotions that are later rationally *justified*.

Moreover, emotion is arguably necessary in order for a decision even to be made. Researchers have carried out experiments proving that certain people are able to properly and rationally analyze different alternatives, but are unable to decide between those alternatives because they lack the requisite emotional response. Dr. Antonio Damasio, professor of neuroscience at the University of Southern California, analyzed this pathology through a patient who had all his cognitive abilities in perfect condition, but who suffered from serious problems in the parts of the brain responsible for managing emotion. According to Damasio, the patient was able to spend 20 minutes listing the advantages and disadvantages of different restaurant choices, but unable to come to any concrete conclusion. "The reason why they cannot decide is because they lack the drive that comes from emotion,"[5] he explained. "It is precisely emotion which allows you to identify different options as good, bad or indifferent. . . . When we think back on past decisions, we usually remember if we felt good or bad about that decision, not just the facts. When we join these two elements—facts and the emotions that come along with them—we are left with what we call wisdom." In this sense, then, emotion is an absolutely necessary requirement for decision making.

At the same time, emotions can complicate and even hamper decision making. Rudy Giuliani, for instance, told me:

> *My father taught me to remain calm in a crisis, because the person that remains calm has enough time to think of the solution. The person who gets very emotional, gets very upset and panics, doesn't see the door that is open and instead sees the five that are closed. The person that remains calm sees the door that is open.*

As we said in Chapter 2, many emotions can undermine our cognitive capacities and therefore limit or disrupt our decision-making capabilities. Giuliani's father was a fireman, so he knew this very, very well. Even the door example he uses comes from his father's experience in fighting fires. In a dangerous emergency situation, you must keep your emotions under control so that you can make a potentially lifesaving decision.

Recognizing Impact and Managing Your Team's Emotions

Positive or negative, emotions are not only a fundamental part of decision making, but also a determining factor in the decisions' final impact—and whether the emotional impact will be negative or positive. Once you realize the emotional impact that the decision-making system has on all members of the company, it becomes clear why it is such an important leadership tool and why it is so important to recognize the emotional impact that decision making and decisions themselves have on teams.

Think about it. By definition, before a decision can be made, there are multiple options. These alternatives evoke different emotions in each member of the team. Each team member will ask herself, "What's going to happen?" "Where are we going?" "Are we going to choose the best option?" and so on. They may feel distress because they don't know what will happen, uncertainty about the future, fears or doubts because the situation lacks clarity, a desire to take on a prominent role, or the fear of losing that role. These emotions then drive the opinions and actions of each individual member of a team; of course, these emotional reactions are as varied and individual as the team members. Therefore, before any decision can be made, there are always contradictory opinions and, thus, the possibility for conflict. Who will prevail? An unmade decision will generate an unclear, uncertain space, bringing a set of negative emotions along with it.

Once a decision is made, however, uncertainty and all other options disappear. The crossroads becomes a straight line toward the next milestone, toward the next crossroads. It doesn't matter that much if the decision is right or wrong, or even if it is the one that certain members of the team would have preferred. Once a decision has been made, it aligns the team behind a goal, establishes a plan, clarifies tasks, simplifies the conversation, and does away with the current crossroads. Once a decision has been made, each team member feels a sense of relief because an emotional weight has been lifted off of their shoulders.

This relief is precisely the opposite of the weight that the leader carries on his shoulders. For a leader, each decision is weighty because not only is it often difficult to make, but, more, a leader is responsible for the impact of a decision's consequences on those around him. He bears the weight of the decision and its consequences on his shoulders. But the ability to handle the emotional strain of the impact of your decisions is what differentiates a true leader from the rest of the pack. As we learned in Chapter 4, President Clinton insists that when leaders realize the impact their decisions have on people, they should not feel paralyzed, but empowered. His ideas warrant repeating. He stresses that we must *"imagine the impact of everything we [say] and [do] on someone else. That's what a leader needs to do, and the best leaders can do it and not be paralyzed by it but be empowered by it."*

The Importance of Self-Confidence When Making Tough or Unpopular Decisions

As this suggests, beyond being aware of and managing the emotional impact of decision making on your team, it is crucial as a decision-making leader to manage your own emotions. In order to illustrate this, it's perhaps easiest to use extreme examples: leaders who face tough decisions. When I ask executives attending my conferences around the world about tough decisions, the response always has to do with a significant emotional impact. Why is that? Because people need to be accepted, loved. They need to be accepted by society as a whole, by the company, by their surrounding subordinates or bosses. There is an innate need for acceptance in every human being, and every decision can put us in danger regarding this. If I make a huge mistake, I fear people will be angry with me, reject me, and exclude me from the group. Unconsciously, it implies that our belonging to the tribe is at risk. It is, therefore, natural that we feel distress about tough decisions.

In the case of politicians, this need for acceptance inevitably runs into the problem of dealing with "popular or unpopular" measures. Former U.K. Prime Minister Tony Blair told me that the hardest part about being a leader is doing the right thing, even if it's not the most popular or obvious option. Thinking back on his own experience during a long conversation I had with him at Radio City Music Hall, Blair explained:

*When I came to politics—I became leader of the
Labour Party in 1994 and then Prime Minister in
1997—I was very much of the school, if I am honest
about it, of "I am going to try and please all the
people all the time," and by the time I left, I wasn't
sure I was pleasing any of the people anytime.*

Blair realized that you cannot be a good leader if you are constantly trying to please everyone, because this keeps you from making the right decisions. If a leader needs others' approval, he will not be able to make proper decisions. That's why he then said:

*Anybody who is in a position of leadership
would have to have sufficient confidence
without that tipping over into arrogance.*

Politicians must be sufficiently confident and emotionally competent to bear the emotional pressure of rejection, to deal with the fact that many people may be angry with the decisions they make. Indeed, all leaders must be self-confident enough to say, in Blair's words:

*Someone has to take responsibilities on their
shoulders. Someone has to make the decision,
and I am going to make the decision.*

If a leader is self-confident, he will be able to make tough decisions without relying on others' approval.

When Colin Powell talks about the most difficult decisions of his career, he makes particular mention of the Gulf War. His bosses were the political leaders responsible for making decisions, but they had to hear his expert opinion on the topic beforehand, "whether they liked it or not." Powell frequently found himself in a position where his bosses wished to hear one thing, but his opinion was likely to be the opposite. However, his responsibility was to deliver his opinion even when he knew it might be unpopular. That's what it is to be a leader even when you are not ultimately the boss. This situation can be a lonely one, and the emotional pressure of having to tell your boss something that he doesn't want to hear can be immense.

That's one of the reasons the best decision makers are those with higher self-esteem. This kind of person's judgment will not be clouded by the need to please others, by a fear of disappointing them, or by the fear of being rejected by them. That's why leaders must also develop their teams' self-esteem—as we saw in the previous section—as well as their own: to be able to stand the pressure of tough decisions. Teams shouldn't be afraid whether a decision is popular or unpopular! In fact, when I asked Bill Clinton, Tony Blair, Colin Powell, and former United States secretary of state Madeleine Albright about the main characteristics they looked for when choosing subordinates, all four mentioned the ability to express opinions different from their boss's and to be ready to face them with different points of view. This implies having enough self-confidence to say what no one wants to hear.

Implicit in the fear of expressing an unpopular opinion or making an unpopular decision is a fear of consequences—another emotion that can play a big role in decision making. Ultimately, emotions affect decision makers' ability to make the right decision because they fear the consequences. Take, for instance, the situation stockbrokers frequently find themselves in. In a conversation with a current trader, I found out what those in that industry mean when they talk about "deciding under pressure." According to this trader, "pressure" in the stock world means the distress and fear of losing everything or of not making enough money. The broker explains:

> When a person has a certain bond and the value starts to drop, it's quite common for him to hold on to it for an irrational amount of time. Because if he sells it, he has to take responsibility for any losses, and that's scary. On the other hand, if he holds on to it, he's delaying that moment. Similarly, when stockbrokers have a bond that starts going up in value, they have a tendency to sell it very quickly to make a profit because they are afraid of losing money. Psychologically, it's very difficult.

MANAGING UNCONSCIOUS INFORMATION: INTUITION AND JUDGMENT

According to chess grandmaster and world chess champion Garry Kasparov, emotion and intuition are among the most important factors in decision making:

> While we make decisions, each person must understand their reactions and their internal mechanisms, which are always unique. To me, emotions are a vital part of this process, as important as intuition, data analysis capacity, or any other factor.

He then added:

> *Intuition is crucial. Some people are not very comfortable relying on their intuition, and I recommend them to train it, like a muscle. You can't improve your intuition unless you rely on it.*

The first time I heard Kasparov's point of view, I was quite surprised. As an engineer, my training had led me to believe—allow me to exaggerate a bit—that anything that cannot be measured or rationalized does not exist. How could intuition possibly play a key role in a game as rational as chess? Kasparov went on to tell me how he had decided to play against Deep Blue in his famous match against the IBM computer. He said that when playing Deep Blue, he tried to use moves that were ambiguous, that left no clear best responses. Using that tactic, he was able to play in ways where he could use his intuition at the last minute.

Even in less extreme situations, intuition is a very important part of the decision-making process. As all of one's unconscious cognitive and emotional capacity, it represents a cumulative foundation or fountain of wisdom from which one draws, most times without even being aware of it. In fact, many specialists on the subject have concluded that intuition is nothing more than the set of experiences and knowledge that a person has gathered in his or her brain, which can be accessed in an unconscious rather than a conscious way. As a result, these experts have found that "sleeping on" a decision, and thus accessing one's unconscious accumulation of information and emotions, helps people to make better decisions.

Filmmaking legend Francis Ford Coppola clearly agrees with this assessment:

In the end, your own intuition, if you have learned to keep it alive and hear its voice, will provide the important answers to critical decisions. I try to make important decisions by relaxing, without getting tense. I think you arrive at the best decisions when you are drinking a glass of wine or in the middle of the night. I don't rush decisions. I hear my colleagues and my assistants, but if it doesn't "click" in my heart, I don't do it. Ultimately, that's what I have.

As you can see, then, intuition is not some mystical quality. Rather, it is the exploitation of everything stored and processed by the subconscious, both emotionally and rationally. If you "keep it alive," as Ford Coppola marvelously put it, it will come to you and help you arrive at a decision—that "click."

Many great leaders agree that the most important decisions cannot be put into a model or a computer, nor can they be made entirely based on reason or consciousness. The most important decisions call for a series of very complex comparisons and assessments that require experience, wisdom, great humility, intuition, and the ability to put several different factors in perspective. One might call this good judgment. In fact, when they describe the world's greatest leaders, many leaders repeat the phrase "good judgment." But what do they mean? Carly Fiorina insists:

Something that shouldn't change is that leadership in the end requires judgment, perspective, insight. If a leader can't make a right judgment on when to move and when to pause, if they don't have the right perspective on what's really important and what's just interesting, then they'll drive the wrong priorities.

As I suspect you're beginning to glean from the words of Kasparov, Fiorina, and Ford Coppola, in the end the importance of intuition and good judgment are not just that they help you make the best decision, but, even more, that they help you make *your* decision.

MAKE *YOUR* DECISION

All decisions are implicitly risky, and, in many cases, it is difficult or impossible to compare the risks of one decision with those of another. Take, for example, Thomas Alva Edison, who created the lightbulb after more than 1,000 attempts. After having "failed" 999 times, who was in a position to say whether a new trial was the right or wrong choice? The inventor didn't care much whether the decision was the "best" or optimum one; it was simply *his decision*, driven by his huge desire to find a solution to his challenge.

It is key that you stop seeking "optimal decisions" or "the best decisions" and start seeking *your own decisions*. Now, this recommendation clearly does not seek to dismiss any models or mechanisms that help us understand the impact of decisions taken, but it does serve as a way to focus on the "North" that we want to attain.

Crisis Management: Run Toward the Problem!

Run to the problem. So if you have a crisis, run to it. Don't avoid it; don't run away from it; don't hide it; run to it. Run to it. Identify it. Acknowledge it. Deal with it.
—**Carly Fiorina**

As you might guess, for leaders the importance and necessity of making *your* decision arises most often and most clearly in moments of crisis, and, unfortunately, it is the rare company and leader who do not face, at some point in their career, a crisis. The word *crisis* comes from the Greek words for "choice" and "alternatives." In other words, a crisis is, in essence, a situation that requires leadership to make critical decisions and choose between various alternatives that will have a huge impact. In fact, decisions during a crisis often define whether an organization will survive or fail. In light of that, the key elements to managing a group in times of crisis are, first, making your decision and having the self-esteem and the courage to bear the emotional weight of that decision and, second, being determined to take charge and "go down into the trenches" to make sure it happens and to support your team.

President Clinton told me:

> *It is always hard to make unpopular decisions, but for me they were not the hardest because I was willing to be judged by the results. The toughest ones were the ones that I had to make within a certain time frame and did not have a clear answer. If the answer was clear, I didn't care if it was popular or unpopular.*

He continues:

> *Ninety percent of the decisions that a president gets credit for making, you check a box on a one-page memo because all of your advisors agree and when you see their analysis it seems self-evident. . . . You really hire the*

president for the other ten percent. The most difficult ones were those where nobody could know the answer. You just had to listen, feel, and do the best thing you could. . . . I made that Mexico decision [on the 1994–1995 debt crisis] in five minutes in spite of my advisors because I was convinced. What killed me was when I had to make a decision that would affect you, and I couldn't be sure that it would be right, but [it] had to be made in a certain time.

As a leader, you are often proceeding without a clear picture of what is going on, without a clear answer as to the consequences, and frequently in the face of the advice and opinion of others. Yet you must make a decision. You are responsible for making a decision—right or wrong—and also for deciding who will benefit and who will suffer. In those moments, the leader is extremely alone because he must consider—or choose to ignore—the interests of each person around him, in addition to establishing, with his decision, who will love and hate him for his actions—popular or unpopular. Considering this, we can think back to Clinton's words on the two emotions that a leader faces when making a decision: he can be paralyzed or motivated by it. Your reaction in these times of crisis determines the kind of leader you are.

Take Rudy Giuliani's handling of the crisis following the September 11 terrorist attacks. He highlights that, at that point in time, he was unable to make decisions as he usually did:

I was always used to hearing this side, then the other; hear it two more times and then decide. Well, here I was hearing one side and then deciding. . . . Three

(continued)

> *minutes later I'd start thinking, "We didn't consider this; we didn't consider that" . . . and I was feeling uncomfortable that I was making the wrong decisions.*

With no time to think and complex and shifting information, Giuliani was nonetheless asked to decide. He could have frozen; instead, he knew he had to go forward.

In times of crisis, leaders not only make decisions in the face of great uncertainty and have the resources to bear the emotional weight, but they also go down into the trenches to be with their teams and support them. After the terrorist attacks on the Twin Towers, Rudy Giuliani did what most great military leaders do. On numerous occasions, particularly in the week following the attacks, he would be found at Ground Zero alongside rescue workers and other officials, sometimes attempting to rally them, other times weeping and mourning alongside them. What real impact do these acts have? First of all, they have an emotional impact. In moments of danger, having the top leader by your side, worrying about you and trying to solve whatever problems may arise, makes you feel safer. You feel important and cared for. This act also shortens information time lag and the decision-making processes. When a leader goes into the trenches, which is where the action is taking place, he will receive all of the relevant information in real time, in the right context, and without any filter; obviously this vastly improves the decision-making process.

Dilemmas of Choice

What about less catastrophic situations, the kinds of problems or conflicts that a business leader might face multiple times over the course of a career? What guides a decision then? For instance, what happens when two major decision-making criteria conflict, such as when fulfilling the organization's vision runs headlong into a problem with ensuring the well-being of the staff? First, you should carefully examine whether the conflict between these criteria is real or just apparent. There is only an apparent conflict when people reject a sacrifice they've been asked to make because they do not see the medium- or long-term benefits of the decision, whereas the leader understands the cost and is considering the medium- and long-term benefits for the group. In that case, even if my staff dislikes my decision—I make an unpopular decision—it doesn't mean that I'm not actually taking care of them. In this apparent conflict, I stay true to the vision and I still take care of my people, regardless of their understanding or adherence.

A different case is when some people bear a cost, but the majority benefits from the decision to try to achieve the vision. An example of this is when you have to lay off some people to ensure the survival and continuity of an organization. Here there is a genuine conflict, but moving toward the organization's vision should have priority over the well-being of a few because the main role of a leader is to establish that vision, direction, and purpose; all decisions must be a step on the path to reaching that objective, so vision is more important than a few followers' specific interests.

Of course, there are managers and entrepreneurs who want to have everything, who consider each person's opinion and only seek consensus and satisfaction, even at the expense of progress. As you might suspect, situations of this sort often have to do with a conflict between the correct measure and the popular decision—and therefore with the emotional difficulty of making an unpopular decision or going against a greater consensus in the name of what is ultimately better. How a leader handles dilemmas of this sort is largely determined by the criterion that he uses when making decisions. Should the leader govern according to what people approve of or according to what he truly believes to be best for the organization, that which will bring the company closer to fulfilling its vision?

During dilemmas, true leaders are guided by two criteria: the vision for the organization and their own decision based on the truth as they see it. To begin with, true leaders move steadily forward guided by vision, convinced that the greater the passion to attain the vision, the easier it is to make decisions that do not please everyone. If your vision and objective are present and strong, you will be able to make unpopular decisions without being affected by the consequences. That's why the majority of successful leaders are unshaken by the prospect of losing some allies while they continue to pursue the company's vision. The leader compensates for the emotional weight of people who do not approve of him or even strongly dislike him with the excitement and energy of getting closer to the collective dream. Only weak leaders are overly concerned with popularity polls.

Second, the leader is responsible for doing what he believes to be correct. This is exactly what Tony Blair so beautifully expresses:

> *If you are in a position of leadership, what you owe people that you are leading, what you owe them in the ultimate analysis, is truth as you see it and the right decision as you perceive it.*

For a true leader, the correct decision must first be illuminated by "the truth as he sees it."

Must We Seek Consensus?

You'll have certainly noticed that a significant portion of our discussion on decision making has to do with a single individual leader making her personal decision, nearly unilaterally. But, as we know, no leader operates in a vacuum; in reality, any leader is surrounded by and responsible to numerous people—their voices, their needs. That's why another factor in making our own decisions has to do with the extent to which we seek consensus. Is consensus a value? Perhaps surprisingly, most of the leaders I've interviewed don't think so, though the directness with which they will state this often varies significantly!

Rather than seeking consensus, most leaders talk about the convenience of having a participatory framework that allows them to listen to all opinions and gather information from a number of sources. As Giuliani explains:

> *Being a leader is not about giving orders, but creating participation. It's about getting the buy-in from people that work with you, that work for you, and people you are working for.*

Getting the team to "buy in" to the decision that is taken is very important because it aligns people behind the proposed action. Don't, however, mistake getting buy-in with consensus; they are not the same. As the mayor implies, a leader needs to get buy-in for a decision he himself has ultimately made—this does not mean the decision made is one arrived at through consensus. When it's time to decide, leaders are the ones who determine whether they trust expert and majority opinions, or whether they prefer to follow their own instincts. The person who is ultimately responsible has to decide if he believes in the delegation system that he has set up, or if he needs to intervene and carry the weight of the decision's consequences on his own shoulders.

Colin Powell echoes these ideas when discussing his "participatory" leadership system, which facilitates the flow of "soft" information—in this case, his subordinates' genuine opinions:

> *I have tried very hard to use a participatory style. I would bring junior officers into my office when I was the head of the Armed Forces, and I would never have my big suit on with all the ribbons and stars; I would just wear a sweater, so that they were relaxed and at ease. I would never use a square table that had somebody at the head; it would always be a round table because I wanted to get the best information out of them, and so I wanted it to be a participatory environment. Now, I also wanted it clear, and this is an important part of leadership that I didn't touch on, that once I have participated and heard what you think, now I am the general, and I will make a decision.*

Powell fosters interactions and gets all the different points of view from his team, but in the end he makes or approves the decisions that are made. Similarly, Jack Welch believes in the importance of participatory management styles, but he adds a firm caveat: *"It was clear to me that it was not a democracy."*

I agree that consensus is not a top-priority value. On critical issues a leader should make sure that everyone contributes with the relevant information and expert opinion necessary; a decision should be made only after hearing from all the experts and leveraging their expertise. But a leader ends up making his decision. It should be one that taps your intuition and benefits from all your knowledge and experience, a decision that clicks in your heart. Whether it is popular or unpopular, has significant or no consensus. You can work later to align the team behind it—the "buy-in." The relevant challenge is to make sure that you make your own decision, that that decision represents your values, and that you lead your people closer to the ultimate vision. By doing so, you make a powerful statement as a leader.

CONCLUSION: DECISION MAKING
AS A LEADERSHIP TOOL

What conclusion can I come to after having explored all these aspects of decision making?

When I make decisions that are in line with my values and my vision and when I focus on decisions that are in line with and reflect the company culture, I'm actually strengthening my team. The delegation system I use helps me create positive states of mind and pushes people to learn and grow as individuals and leaders. It empowers them, and when I empower people through smart decision-making systems, I'm ensuring the success of the organization. I'm boosting my employees' self-esteem, their commitment to the organization, their progress toward the common dream, and their sense of belonging in a group that makes decisions based on clear criteria.

But as clear as you may think your decision-making criteria and processes are, emotions play an enormous role in decision making, and most people are not even aware of the role their emotions play—not before, during, or after the actual making of decisions. Similarly, you need to recognize and train your own intuition, which is an unconscious process that takes into account both information and emotions stored in your brain. It is the capacity to instinctively *feel* a better choice. Becoming aware of these processes will enable you to make better decisions.

Managing all of the diverse aspects of the decision-making system that we have reviewed in this chapter is an incredibly effective tool to develop and inspire talent! To invite you to reflect on whether you are leveraging decision making as a leadership tool, I want to close this chapter with the following question:

> *Are you empowering your team to help each member grow in self-esteem, confidence, and commitment by giving them increasing responsibilities and enabling them to make informed, supported decisions?*

CHAPTER 7

FIFTH ROLE: UNDERSTANDING, CREATING, AND MANAGING YOUR CULTURE—THE CULTURE PLAN

We have to hire and fire people based on [our] values.

—Tony Hsieh

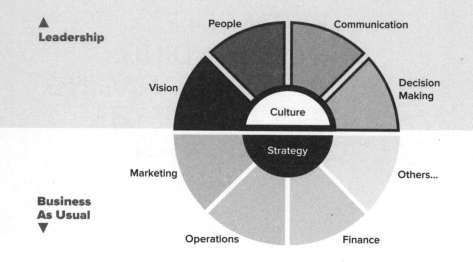

Leadership ▲

People Communication

Vision Decision Making

Culture

Strategy

Marketing Others...

Business As Usual ▼

Operations Finance

In the previous four chapters, we analyzed the first four roles the Chief Emotions Officer must embody and how she uses these roles to generate specific states of mind and emotions. Each role had a series of concrete emotional results that could be perceived or measured, and, often, a role focused on generating one or two specific emotions. Let's take a brief look back at these:

- Inspiring a vision results in people having the positive emotions that guarantee success, such as a sense of purpose, pride, commitment, passion, hope, and happiness.

- Caring about and taking care of people results in them having a sense of belonging, pride, engagement, commitment, self-esteem, self-confidence, and even trust.

- Communication across the organization results particularly in creating the connections that build trust.

- A strong decision-making system drives empowerment and results chiefly in growing self-esteem and self-confidence.

I would say that these first four leadership roles are individual. Each person has her own dream and vision and can genuinely take care of the people around her; each person can communicate and connect with her team effectively and create a decision-making system that empowers people. But individual leadership variables are always displayed through the group's culture, which is why the fifth role, understanding and managing organizational culture, refers to groups.

UNDERSTANDING *YOUR*
ORGANIZATIONAL CULTURE

In distinction from the broader beliefs, customs, and behaviors that make up culture in general, I use the term *organizational culture* to refer to the set of values and behaviors that differentiate a smaller group of people, such as those found in a company, department, or business unit. The particular values and behaviors of that organizational culture guide its emotions and energy toward a common dream and make its members feel that they belong to a community. Indeed, organizational culture is everything that causes the people in an organization to experience certain emotions and states of mind as they strive to achieve a common vision. One could even argue that the organizational culture arises from the emotional impact created by a unified dream and a common set of values and behaviors.

For example, Carlos Brito says that AB InBev's organizational culture is the same in every country it operates in. The company's values are the same all around the world, no matter what the broader culture may be. As we briefly mentioned earlier and will see in more detail later this chapter, AB InBev's culture is about "being owners" and behaving like owners, so, whether it's in India or the United States, this culture guides everything from employee behaviors and communication to decision making, thereby ensuring that consumers get the same level of service and the same quality product wherever they are and that employees from Boston to Bombay follow the same company dream and behave according to the same values and behaviors.

Sure, most international companies don't say they have *exactly* the same culture regardless of where they are; local iterations, of course, require small modifications. Nonetheless, we can certainly understand how organizational culture helps a business maintain its overall identity no matter where it is. Doing so is a fundamental necessity in this age of global industry and global brands: by helping a business to keep its identity across broader cultural boundaries, organizational culture breeds the trust necessary to sustain customer loyalty and greater global success, as well as to bolster internal pride and sense of belonging.

Of course, an organization's culture is undeniably immersed in the larger societal culture in which the organization is found, and therefore naturally incorporates certain elements of the broader culture while having to reckon with others. AB InBev, for instance, may choose to have the same values wherever it operates, but the impact that those values have on people in different countries will surely be quite dissimilar. Take as an example an organizational culture that expects full-time employees to work upwards of 60 hours a week without extra compensation and simply in order to maintain their positions. This may be a pill too bitter for a French worker to swallow without revolt, whereas an American worker in a highly competitive firm may see this less as an exception than as a norm and quietly go on.

Let's look at the relationship between greater cultural values and those of a company's organizational culture from the perspective of generational differences and examine it in light of a broad cultural trend that has had a pronounced impact on organizational culture: the emergence of *millennials* into the workforce. Born between approximately 1981 and 1995, millennials work in a very different way than previous generations because they exalt a particular set of values: a work-life balance, caring for the planet, the fostering of social well-being, and short-term projects. With each passing year, it becomes more and more important for companies to thoroughly analyze and understand the unique values and expectations of the new generation in order to successfully manage the company's organizational culture—particularly when attempting to attract and hold onto new talent. If, for example, you want millennials to identify with and commit to your company, they must perceive the organization as willing to provide the conditions necessary for them to have time for other personal activities. In addition, the company should show a high level of respect for the environment and initiatives that seek to improve social well-being. Moreover, unlike previous generations, millennials are not so drawn to job stability and long-term projects. Unless a company takes into account and respects general millennial values, it should be ready to lose its most valuable talent—if it can attract it in the first place!

In a recent keynote speech for one of the top Latin American law firms, a partner was complaining that the firm was having difficulties attracting young talent. I asked him about the firm's dreams and vision and what purpose it was trying to invite young talent to join. He answered, "Our basic value is working hard, and through hard work we are trying to achieve excellence." I think that answer explains why they were having trouble getting young talented people. Millennials just don't see hard work in and of itself as a value, especially if it is not in pursuit of a strongly believed purpose.

As you can see, it is crucial that companies understand the larger sociocultural context in which they are operating, because this context will have a great influence on the values and behaviors found in those who make up the workforce. Therefore, the values that a company chooses to make up its organizational culture must be in line with those greater cultural values that the workforce adheres to. This starts at the very top!

CULTURE STARTS AT THE TOP

*I didn't know this when I became CEO, but everything
I do is a reinforcement of what we want to do
culturally. . . . The tone at the top in terms of values,
culture and what's important is non-delegable. You can
coach other people but the culture, the transformation
and standing up for it, believing in it, teaching it,
that starts with the CEO. You can delegate anything
you want, but you cannot delegate culture.*[1]
—**Steve Ballmer,** CEO of Microsoft, 2000–2014

Because organizational culture is a shared vision and a set of common values and behaviors for everyone in the organization, senior leaders must share the culture, above all. The higher you are in the organization, the bigger your impact in defining your corporate culture. So, if you are the CEO, before anyone else, you must embody the organizational culture you want to spread throughout. Then you have to work closely with your top management team to make sure that everyone is aligned behind that culture. Even if the leaders of an organization have certain individual differences, it is crucial that they work together to build common elements across several dimensions and then behave in a way that reinforces the culture expressed in these common elements.

Top leadership can (and should) consciously and actively promote a positive culture. But organizational culture is ultimately the result of how people in the organization *actually* behave and feel. As such, the leadership can just as easily create a destructive or exploitative culture. For instance, if culture is not properly managed, a particular manager with more attractive proposals, actions, or personal abilities may gain greater influence in the organization's culture, effectively undoing the positive work and vision of other leaders.

I once heard the founding partner of a company say that his product was an empty promise, only of value to idiots, and that he no longer believed in it. Can you imagine what a huge impact that kind of statement had on the company's people? He also rewarded people who did not live by or respect the organization's values, failed to follow strategic behaviors that had previously led to growth, and abandoned the company's dream. What else is there to say? What kind of company can survive all this? This leader stripped away the value of his own business, which dropped until it almost reached bankruptcy. A once-successful company, which had multiplied its profits four times over in just five years, saw a drop in sales and started suffering losses that would continue for years to come.

All members of an organization have something to contribute to the group's culture, but senior leaders have a greater impact and their role in creating, guiding, and embodying the culture is of the utmost significance. When a founder or head executive no longer believes in the business, he is slowly destroying what the people at the organization worked so hard to create. It is therefore time for that leader to step aside.

DISTINGUISHING DIFFERENT TYPES OF CULTURE

In the first chapter, we focused on the *impact* an organization's culture can make on *results*. I did this because leadership is obliged to get results, so I felt it was important to stress to you early on that culture can make a big difference to a company's success. Actually, leadership can not only get results, but multiply them manyfold by creating a successful culture. That is, all things said, what leaders do: they create cultures, and those cultures can multiply results.

In this section, I want to share with you in more detail different prototypes of cultures so that you can visualize where you are in yours and decide which way you would like to modify it. The focus is more on understanding, for some particularly successful companies, the strategic goals they have and the corresponding values and behaviors that make up their cultures.

In order to ultimately manage one's culture well, it is obviously crucial to first understand and define the primary variables of that culture according to the set of behaviors, values, and habits lived at that company. Today people talk about all different kinds of cultures. There's purpose-driven culture, the culture of innovation, the culture of excellence, the culture of human values, the culture of ownership, cost- or profit-driven cultures, and many others. Let me show here some particular examples of these kinds of cultures.

The Culture of Purpose

Many CEOs make the mistake of thinking that encouraging a "professional culture" is enough to generate constant growth in the company. This scheme may have worked effectively 40 years ago when young professionals were only interested in achieving a successful work life, but the situation nowadays is quite different. As we discussed, millennials are unsatisfied with strictly economic and professional objectives; this new generation of professionals wants to do something meaningful and contribute to policies that strengthen society and lead to real change, from within their companies.

Therefore, companies that only manage the "professional" side of culture are no longer the paradigm or model to follow. To the contrary, they must embrace the enormous opportunity they have to grow by looking beyond this narrow focus. Nowadays, in addition to supplying their products and services, companies should contribute to the general well-being of their members and to that of society as a whole. We could call this focus the *culture of purpose*, or *purpose-driven culture*.

It is important to understand that these objectives—the professionalism devoted to the success of products and services, on the one hand, and, on the other, the commitment to strengthen the general well-being of employees and of society—are not in opposition to one another. Rather, they are mutually reinforcing. If a company chooses to go *beyond* professionalism by also encouraging people's passions and taking care of employees' well-being, it will reinforce its growth and development possibilities. Take, for example, companies like Zappos.com and Southwest Airlines, whose cultures of promoting first-rate service at the same time as they put their employees first has led them to superior business and financial performance. As we saw in the first chapter, Southwest, for instance, yielded an almost 26 percent annual return over a 30-year period! You don't have to be a business analyst to see that's outstanding performance.

Another example of a culture of purpose and people is the microblogging social network Twitter. It began as a start-up with a handful of people working toward a common dream: to reach every person on the planet. Twitter's mission is "To give everyone the power to create and share ideas and information instantly, without barriers." Biz Stone, Twitter's cofounder, explained the significance of the company's culture in accomplishing such an ambitious goal:

> *We were building something that was going to be important in people's lives—not just people who use Twitter, but the people who came and worked at Twitter. And we wanted to be a great place to work, and we wanted people to feel like they were doing meaningful work and the best work of their lives, and we are also responsible for things like their health and things like that. It became clear that a strong culture was going to be important if we were going to continue to grow.*

You'll have noticed that Stone highlights the importance, first, of a greater purpose—the importance of feeling at Twitter that you belong to something great and that you are making a deep impact on the world—and, second, of caring for the people that belong to the company. These two aspects are the cornerstones of purpose- and people-driven cultures and companies, and they have helped Twitter to become one of the world's most powerful social networks and economic successes—with quarterly earnings close to $250 million and more than 250 million users in 2014.

The Culture of Results

In order to understand what a "culture of results" is and what behaviors and values are necessary to establish it, we must stress, first and foremost, that this kind of culture requires a precise definition of the way we will measure results—whether it is in terms of sales, client growth, company profits, consumer satisfaction or any other appropriate metric. The factor chosen will serve as a guide in developing the company's specific "culture of results," which differentiates it from others; for instance, if our culture relies on measuring results in terms of sales, this factor will produce a culture distinct from one based on, say, customer satisfaction. The particular defining "result" chosen then becomes the dream of the entire organization.

Bob Herbold's experience provides us with a very interesting illustration of a culture of results based on a specific factor. After 26 years of working at Procter & Gamble, Herbold received a personal call from Bill Gates to discuss the business challenges that Microsoft was facing, particularly with profitability and innovation. After meeting with Gates a few times, Herbold started working at Microsoft. Over the course of the 10 years he stayed there, Herbold instituted a culture of results, where the primary measurement factor was profit—and he did this with great success, helping to increase Microsoft's profits sevenfold during his seven-year tenure as executive vice president and chief operating officer.

How did he create a successful culture of results where the main factor was profit? Later, when asked about his experience with the information giant, Bob responded with three simple words: *"Creativity and discipline. . . . Those are two key drivers of profitability,"* he explained, *"discipline and creativity. Disciplined to the extreme means there's no creativity. An extremely creative enterprise has difficulty being disciplined. Obviously what you need is the right kind of balance."* On the one hand, he more rigorously organized the company's accounting and IT systems, which allowed him to lower costs, and, on the other hand, he established flexible guidelines for areas oriented toward developing products and services that would excite customers and benefit the company. By establishing a balance between disciplined accounting and flexible creativity, Herbold was able to build a culture where innovation increased profitability, the end goal. Indeed, a culture of results means aligning everything in the culture to attain those predefined results.

The Culture of Ownership

We don't like the words "executives" or "professionals"; we like the word "owners." Why? Because owners make better decisions because it's their company: "It's my company; I am going to be here to take the consequences." A lot of companies hire a guy from the market; that's a shortcut. Of course he comes with 10 years of experience, but this guy comes with a different set of values, a different culture. And then the fabric that took 20 years to build is going to be diluted. And that's not the way to do it.
—**Carlos Brito**

Although Brito initially became famous as a CEO for his results at Anheuser-Busch InBev—in 2012 it had a 39 percent margin, up from 31 percent in 2008, while SABMiller, its main competitor, reported an EBITDA margin of 23 percent[?]—he was later applauded for his "culture of ownership" concept. To describe this culture, where the focus is on mindset, on how people do everything they do, Brito uses the example of the different behaviors exhibited by a car owner and a car renter. Whereas people who rent a car tend to be careless with the product, people driving their own car are generally much more careful when on the road. According to Brito, this is the difference between having conventional employees and those who feel that they "own" the company:

> You wouldn't like it if an employee treated the company as they would treat a rental car. So, creating that feeling of ownership is going to ensure that when an employee makes a decision, he will do so with the company's interests in mind, instead of his own personal interests.

If I am able to make all members of my organization, from top to bottom, fulfill their responsibilities, while also feeling responsible for everything that happens there, I will have created a powerful culture. To do this, Brito explains, you must work with your people to generate a sense of belonging that carries with it a sense of responsibility to the whole.

Think Like an Owner

Clearly, every employee in a company that espouses a culture of ownership must think and act as though she were the owner— that is, take an interest in and responsibility for the company as though it were her very own. Yes, if you want employees to behave like owners, they have to think like them. Here's how you can encourage this.

The Owner Looks at the Big Picture
Vision and Takes Responsibility

The owner sees the big picture and is able to recognize that all parts serve the entire organization. If the owner sees a sheet of paper on the floor, he doesn't think, "I'm not responsible for picking that up." If he sees a sad employee or an out-of-order bathroom, he doesn't think, "I'll let someone else be responsible for that." Why? Because he is responsible for everything, even if he ultimately has to delegate some responsibilities.

I actually believe that job descriptions could in fact be one of the most harmful management tools when it comes to encouraging a culture of ownership. Why? Because in defining "my little garden," they exclude everything else. They strongly suggest that everything that happens outside my well-defined little plot does not concern me. An owner, on the other hand, has no job description or private "garden" to look after because his responsibilities span the entire business or company.

Yes, an organization may determine that certain people are responsible for solving certain issues or carrying out certain tasks, but the responsibility for identifying and assessing these issues and tasks should not be limited to just one person or sector. That's why I think that it is important to understand a job description in a new and perhaps unorthodox way: a job description defines the things that one must "do," but all members of the organization should be responsible for proposing ideas that take into account the entire organization, as well as keeping an eye out for any issues.

The Owner Has a Long-Term Vision

Owners think in the long term because they will be there to deal with future results. In contrast, employees commonly concentrate on the impact that their decisions will have while they are in charge, which means that they often have short- or medium-term expectations and make short- or medium-term choices because, especially these days, they won't be there for the long haul. Time and time again, I have seen executives of multinational companies—who are just highly paid employees—make short-term decisions regarding investment, spending, and hiring; since these bosses only spend two or three years in their position before moving on to a new country or region, they only worry about the impact these decisions will have while they are working at that job in the organization, ignoring any future impact. In a culture of ownership, all employees would do their best to act with long-term consequences in mind.

The Owner Has Flexibility Beyond Standard Procedures

Owners don't tend to have as rigidly defined guidelines and procedures for behavior as employees do; they can be more flexible in order to please the customer. If, for example, a customer arrives five minutes after a restaurant's lunch service has wrapped up, rather than telling him that the kitchen has already closed, the owner will tell him to wait a minute to see what he can offer him. The owner makes exceptions because he knows that guidelines are there just for that, to guide, but if you want to maintain high standards in terms of customer service and develop greater profits, you sometimes need to go beyond the norms. Think back to our Southwest Airlines example and the employee who hired the buses!

Of course, there are many examples of employees that behave like owners. On a recent trip to Bogotá, Colombia, I arrived at the Sheraton hotel and went to the front desk to check in. I was quite surprised when a waiter came over with a tray of drinks and said, "Welcome! Would you like a glass of lemonade?" Whether it was the waiter's personal initiative or a cultural dictate handed down by his boss, the waiter behaved with the typical welcoming behavior of an owner. This incident would have met with Brito's approval, as it crystallizes his philosophy for the culture of owner-ship. Here, the waiter plays the role of host and owner in order to ensure the customer's satisfaction and contributes to the success of the hotel overall.

The Owner Cares About Results and Creating Value

One of the consequences of thinking about the big picture, long-term results, and being flexible toward the customer is that the owner becomes quite aware of how value is created and which actions lead to which results. The owner knows that each job is actually a link in a bigger chain, so he must be aware of how one job integrates into other jobs and turns into results and value to the client. In an ideal environment—in a culture of owner-ship—an employee would demonstrate a similar familiarity with the relation between his job and others in the overall production process to create value and results. An employee would behave as though she were the owner.

The Culture of Innovation

If innovation was important, we had to measure it.
So I said, "OK, we are actually going to measure
innovation." We measured it in a variety of ways. But
one of the ways we did it was in patent production.
And by the time I left, we were generating 11 patents a
day. And we had gone from not even being on the list
of the top 25 innovators in the world to being number
three. That's important for a technology company.
—**Carly Fiorina**

From a corporate point of view, it would appear that innovative companies are the modern Holy Grail or the secret to eternal youth, and with this goal in mind, a large part of management literature has focused on processes for new products or services and new business models as key variables to become innovative.

I agree that all organizations must be innovative, but I believe that the key to *constant* innovation isn't a matter of *processes*, but mainly of *culture*. The real key is to create a culture of innovation because culture not only includes the formation of processes that lead to innovation, but also injects the organization with a spirit, with values and behaviors that have a wider, more effective, and longer-lasting impact on innovation.

World-renowned expert on creativity Sir Ken Robinson also recognizes the importance of creating a culture to the fostering of innovation. He says:

> *Great leaders recognize that if you want to encourage*
> *creativity and innovation, you have to develop talent,*

(continued)

because your job as a leader is not to have all the ideas but to create a culture that allows everyone to have them, [and to] then encourage them to propose those ideas and finally have a process to evaluate them.

That said, what makes a culture innovative? In order to help us identify which values and behaviors make up a successful innovative organizational culture, let's look at an example of one: Procter & Gamble, one of the most powerful companies in the world.

During an interview we did at Rockefeller Center in 2010, A. G. Lafley—executive chairman of Procter & Gamble and former chairman, president, and CEO—told me that before he became the CEO of the company in 2000, only 15 to 20 percent of the products and services launched by P&G were successful, which meant that only one out of every six products received a satisfactory response from consumers. Growing an already huge company in a saturated market is not an easy thing to do; correcting disappointing results such as these can seem nearly impossible. So, when Lafley became CEO, he implemented a culture of innovation as a core component of his plan to generate results and spur growth.

To begin with, Lafley ensured that P&G's highly efficient and motivated employees knew the "consumer is boss" and that they truly adhered to the mission of the company—a mission already firmly grounded in innovation: "Improving more consumers' lives in small but meaningful ways each day." He made sure everyone understood that innovation wasn't meant only for engineers and product developers, but that it had to be a general policy, applicable to every aspect of the business, from the research and development department to customer service, accounting, and financial, among others.

P&G realized that innovation comes from proposals and ideas, which in turn come from people. An organization must, therefore, provide its people with an environment in which they are encouraged to ask questions, to develop and propose ideas, and then have the appropriate processes and capabilities to turn them into new businesses. That environment must stimulate behaviors key to creativity, like curiosity and fostering a spirit of improvement; it must value diversity of knowledge, of backgrounds, and of points of view. The environment that supports innovation must also be built on trust, which is the basis for collaboration, as innovation is always the result of teamwork.

P&G instituted an open innovation practice, developing and taking advantage of the skills of everyone in the company, and finding partners outside P&G that enhanced their own strengths—"Connect + Develop." Plus, in both recruitment and internal professional development, it focused on soft variables, such as agility, flexibility, empathy, and emotional intelligence, so that development and growth became part of people's lives and in order to enhance understanding of consumers' expectations and needs.

Upon the installment of Lafley's culture of innovation, P&G, with its 120,000 employees in more than 80 countries, successfully reduced investment in research and development (from 4.5 percent to 2.8 percent by 2007), increasing revenues and getting more value for each dollar invested. In fact, under Lafley's management, P&G increased its initial product and services success rate from a range of 15 to 20 percent to 50 percent, plainly proving that one of the most important qualities of an innovative culture is an open, fully integrated environment in which invention and improvement can flourish. Furthermore, although Lafley believes that he and his workforce were capable of increasing this percentage even more, he didn't want P&G to become a slave to its own goals and end up opting for "safe" decisions in order to avoid risking failure. As he explained, this "would reduce our ability to change." He realizes that innovation requires one to embrace the risk of failure.

Indeed, most important, in order for a company to innovate, it must take risks, make mistakes, learn from them, make more mistakes, and so on. Yes, encouraging creativity and innovation means tolerating and even embracing "errors" as an absolutely necessary step in the process and recognizing that they are the starting point for all learning. If errors are discouraged, punished, or simply avoided, innovation will be impossible because it will lack the environment it needs to develop. During a recent trip to Germany, for example, I talked with a group of executives who said, *"The biggest challenge we face at Siemens is innovating. Because the company has an engineering culture, everyone tries to do things 'right' from the start, and that isn't good for innovation."* For innovative companies, in contrast, products and services are always in trial mode: they are tested, errors emerge, and the company learns from those mistakes, corrects them, and starts all over again. If experimentation and error are not tolerated, innovation becomes impossible.

Robinson once told me about a friend of his who had won the Nobel Prize in Chemistry. This friend assured him that 98 percent of his experiments had failed. According to Robinson, the Noble Prize winner added that "failure" wasn't the correct word to use when referring to this high percentage, because when you are searching for something that doesn't yet exist, you are constantly experimenting to see what works and what doesn't. Being allowed to fail, explained Robinson, is a very important part of encouraging creativity, so, *"when you find yourself in a company culture where you're afraid to fail, innovation and creative thought start to be obstructed."*

As Ed Catmull, cofounder and president of Pixar and Walt Disney Animation Studios, says in his book *Creativity, Inc.*: "It's better to fix problems than to prevent them all." Michael Eisner, who in 21 years as CEO of Disney transformed the cartoon company into a media conglomerate whose triumphs include, among other things, a partnership with Pixar to produce the ground-breaking hit *Toy Story*, echoes this, insisting that, in order to be successful, you have to *"Be willing to dance with failure."*

Pixar

Let's pause to look more closely at Pixar, one of the most innovative companies in recent years. Pixar's founders shared the dream of creating the first computer-animated feature film, and since realizing this dream with 1995's *Toy Story*, Pixar has not only redefined the animation field and reinvented the animation business; it has also turned itself into a business paradigm. All its animated features have enjoyed blockbuster success. People around the world dream of getting into the magic world responsible for creating the characters in *Finding Nemo*, *Up*, *Monsters, Inc.*, and *The Incredibles*, as well as taking part in an enterprise shaped by state-of-the-art technology and unlimited creativity. So, what is the secret to Pixar's innovation? What goes into a culture that produces such innovative results?

Like P&G, Pixar's culture of innovation is built on its ability to deal with risk by constantly learning from mistakes, its focus on wide-ranging, open collaboration built on trust, and its devotion to the soft variables that demonstrate a true concern for its people.

At the heart of Pixar's fervent culture of innovation, we most certainly find a willingness to "dance with failure." Management's job at Pixar is categorically not to prevent risk, but, rather, to build the capability to recover when failures occur. Movies like *Ratatouille*, in which the main character is a French rat who aspires to be a chef, are so bold or crazy that no one knows if they are going to work beforehand. Pixar wants to provide customers with new experiences every time they go to the movies, and hand in hand with this emphasis on novelty goes artistic as well as technological risk. "We as executives have to resist our natural tendency to avoid or minimize risks," Catmull wrote in an article from the *Harvard Business Review*. "If you want to be original, you have to accept the uncertainty, even when it's uncomfortable, and have the capability to recover when your organization takes a big risk and fails."[3]

"What's the key to being able to recover?" Catmull asks when considering the risk involved with originality. "Talented people!" Contrary to what most people imagine when they think of this kind of company, Pixar does not base its success on cutting-edge technology or a couple of eccentric creative geniuses. Rather, the animated film producer's impressive success and the key to its culture of innovation lie in its unique approach to people. Randy Nelson, former dean of Pixar University, insists on the company's desire to develop its people: "We've made the leap from an idea-centered business to a people-centered business. . . . We're trying to create a culture of learning, filled with lifelong learners."[4]

This promotion of learning and broad-reaching interest has very practical applications at Pixar, where collaboration is the name of the game. Contrary to the commonly accepted belief that a movie is one or two ideas, Catmull stresses how it is all about effective collaboration. Any movie is made up of thousands of ideas that are in every line of the script, the design of every character and background, the angle of the camera, the colors, the lights and the pace; therefore, "The director and the other creative leaders of a production do not come up with all the ideas on their own; rather, every single member of the 200- to 250-person production group makes suggestions."[5]

Because employees' opinions represent different points of views that often end up being complementary, everyone at Pixar is encouraged to give opinions, and employees are sometimes invited to participate in the decision-making process in different areas of the company. In the end, Pixar makes sure its people have the ability and opportunity to participate effectively in groups that can develop ideas and solutions.

That high degree of collaboration takes trust and respect. It must be safe to tell the truth; it must be safe to make mistakes and learn from errors. In his *HBR* article, Catmull points out that Pixar prioritizes collaboration above competition because it believes it is much more important to have a group of people who are open to dialogue and willing to work as a team than to have a few geniuses in different areas who are unable to work together. Pixar cultivates innovation by stressing relationships and building a very strong sense of community.

Crucial to this sense of community and its ability to generate innovation is Pixar's care for the well-being of its people. For example, executives at Pixar try to establish a balance between its employees' work and personal lives. Recognizing that the production of animated movies can require months of absolute dedication, the company compensates by special leaves, sabbaticals, and moments dedicated solely to having fun.

The example of Pixar shows us the values and behaviors of a successful culture of innovation, one made up of a strong community openly collaborating to achieve the company's vision without fear of risk or error because caring has built a platform of trust and security.

The Existence of Subcultures

Of course, in addition to the greater organizational culture of a company, each company has multiple subcultures that emerge as a result of different departments' contexts, functions, challenges, and dreams. Different sectors of an organization should not have different values, and the organization's values should not change much over time, because they are what define and unify the company. However, various divisions can have different strategic behaviors. That is, which specific behaviors the company's values manifest themselves in may differ from department to department depending on that department's particular role within the organization.

The clearest example of subculture that I can think of is the example we spoke of in the last chapter, when Herb Kelleher ripped up Southwest Airlines's 500-page customer service department manual and replaced it with a single page of guidelines. In doing this, the company was seeking to encourage personal responsibility, initiative, creativity, and personal judgment in this department—a department whose role was also central to Southwest's vision of itself as a premier provider of good service. However, in that same company, the maintenance department must follow strict protocols and 500-page manuals. Does this mean that these two departments have two different cultures? No, but they do have two different subcultures. They have the same values and the same vision for the organization, but different behaviors that correspond to two different functions—much in the same way that the accounting department also has its own way of living the company culture.

Whether it's the accounting department, customer service, or maintenance, in order for your employees to embrace your organizational culture, you have to make sure they understand what it is and that you manage it thoughtfully!

THE CULTURE PLAN

*Mostly I saw my role as creating the strategies for
the company, but also [as] creating a culture in
which really talented people would want to come
and work and would do really good work.*
—**Christie Hefner,** former CEO and
chairman, Playboy Enterprises

In my trips around the world to share the lessons I've learned, I've
noticed that everyone has a strategic plan, clearly defining how they
will compete and their stand on all the hard variables. However, I
have very rarely found companies with a *culture plan* that expresses
a clear understanding of the dimensions constituting their culture.
As we said at the beginning of the book, culture is difficult to see
and define, and that is probably why people don't take the time
to identify it, to understand it, and most important, to make sure
that everyone understands it and follows it. However, if you don't
have "committable core values"—that is, values and behaviors by
which you are willing to hire and fire people—if you don't devote
time and attention to managing your culture, it will end up fading
away and you will end up with a staff that is off focus and unable to
attain your goals. So, to really have a culture that multiplies results,
you need to devote a significant amount of time and resources to
understanding that culture, shaping it, and living according to it.
I call this building your *culture plan*. The *culture plan* is a tool to
define, build, and manage a company's organizational culture.

How do you do this? Well, one thing you *shouldn't* do is turn
back a few pages and just borrow aspects from one of the different organizational cultures we have explored or imitate the values
and behaviors selected by well-known CEOs whose particular cultures have led to successful enterprises. The secret to success does

not lie in replicating what other leaders have done, but in choosing the values and behaviors that most closely relate to the vision that your company has established or that you want to establish. Yes, building a culture through the creation of a *culture plan* is all about choosing the values and behaviors that will enable *your* company's vision to take real shape.

The first step in fashioning your culture plan is to review and define all the elements that make up your culture—or the one you wish to create.

Please take a moment to reflect on the following questions:

- What is the company's vision and purpose? Do all members of the organization share the same dream, and is that what gets them out of bed every morning?

- What values and behaviors do I want to embrace? Do the people in my organization or team know how to put those values into action?

- Have I identified, communicated, and rewarded the strategic behaviors that allow me to deliver my value proposition and execute my strategy?

- Does my brand accurately represent that value proposition? What does my brand stand for?

- What are the values and behaviors that I need to cultivate in my company in order to deliver the promise the brand and the culture behind it stand for?

- Do values like candor and keeping your word promote communication and trust-building?

It is crucial that the answers be genuine and true so that, when the results distilled from them are ultimately codified, any member of the organization can respond clearly and spontaneously when asked, "What are the company's values and strategic behaviors?"

Equally important to the creation and development of a culture plan for your company is *your* relation to the values and behaviors embedded there. That is, the organizational values and behaviors that make up the cultural plan must also jibe with the values of the leader. As an exercise to identify your values and the values and behaviors of a culture you might embrace or wish to create, you can follow the great advice of Zappos.com's Tony Hsieh:

> *To know which values you really have, make a list of people you like working with and another with people you don't like working with. Behind each person, write the reason why you like or dislike working with that person. There you will have a first draft of your list of values.*

In addition to Hsieh's list, I would recommend you ask the following things:

- Why does this organization exist? Do I share that dream?

- Do I share the values that drive this organization?

- Does the organizational culture fit me personally? Does my personality fit the culture?

- What do I most like to do? Where do I best develop my potential?

- Why do I jump out of bed every morning to go to work?

- When I get up in the morning, do I feel proud, committed, and happy to work in my organization?

- What could I do—if anything—to make that so?

Why is it so important to the creation of a genuine, comprehensive, and effective culture plan that the values and behaviors of the organization and those of the leader—or indeed any employee—jibe? Because creating and managing culture is not about generating a mechanical, memorized response; on the contrary, it requires that leaders and all other members live by those standards and express them in everyday activities. You just feel those values and embody the behaviors. In fact, for a leader, the only way to ensure that a corporate culture will reach its full potential is to be an example day in and day out, and to actively defend the organization's values and strategic behaviors. Amina Enste-Meineker, creator of the culture consulting firm Corporate Passion, sums this up very well:

Culture is created by how things are actually done— not by what is written on some wall or told in some speech. Consistency is crucial. If you preach respect for the CEO, but then the CEO of the organization uses his smartphone during an interview to check his mail, the message that is transmitted is not respect. Humans have an uncanny "sensor" for what is truly happening: What is actually rewarded? How is making mistakes treated? How are decisions being made? Who gets a say? How do we communicate? And what does all this mean for the performing capacity of all of us as a team? As a group of people who get up every day to work for the same employer—so presumably for the same cause?

Only if you "walk the talk" will you be able to create the positive states of mind and emotions that have led to such outstanding results in other organizations and capture them in your culture plan.

Furthermore, if you are part of the management team, you need to make sure that your culture plan and all that it implies is deeply embedded in all of your management systems.

EMBEDDING YOUR CULTURE IN YOUR MANAGEMENT SYSTEMS

When the organization grows, establish Culture Committees as missionaries to spread the word and keep the fire of culture burning, and constantly honor and celebrate the employees that are the role models for all of your people and how you want them to behave.
—Herb Kelleher

Once you have identified the criteria and values that you wish to define your culture, make sure that they become part of the management systems, that they are put into practice and become part of the day-to-day business culture, and that you have defined all the ways for constantly monitoring them. Here are a few basic guidelines that will help you to implement and manage your organizational culture:

- As we stressed earlier, all members of the company, especially top executives, should commit to the organization's values and criteria, as demonstrated through their exemplary behavior. If leaders do not live by the organization's values and purpose, no one will.

- Make sure your values are formalized and become part of all procedures and processes related to people. Review your recruiting, evaluation, promotion, and firing policies, including incentives, rewards, and bonuses. Your values have to be present in the cafeteria, the hallways, and every corner of the company, and be part of the criteria in every facet of the decision-making process.

- Make sure that information flows in all directions by creating open arenas of communication. Foster trust-building practices like candid communication and keeping your promises.

- Culture is manifested in celebrations: what do we celebrate and what do we reward?

- Establish "Culture Committees," small groups across the organization that will ensure the strengthening of the culture through a myriad of actions.

- All training programs should be coherent with corporate values.

Of the tools in this list, I would like to focus on the importance of recruiting and firing personnel because these two processes have a very powerful impact both on creating culture and on ensuring that the values and attitudes of that culture remain embedded in a high-functioning way in the day to day of the organization.

Hiring: How Can You Take in a Queen Bee?

To illustrate the importance of culture and the culture plan in the role of hiring, consider this. If companies are unable to conceptualize and express the elements of their own culture, they will neither consistently hire candidates that represent that culture nor be able to successfully integrate talent into their culture.

Take the well-known and significant problem of cultural incompatibility in the hiring of top executives. Very often, extremely successful executives in one company fail terribly within months of being hired by another company. The explanation for this phenomenon does not lie in individual professional competency, but in culture. To put it simply, each party—the executive and the organization—has its own culture, and only one of them can survive intact. Sound drastic? Perhaps not as much as you think.

Miguel Ascarate, the COO of Ledesma S.A.A.I., an Argentinian agribusiness whose 2011 revenue was $750 million,[6] once told me that his father, an experienced beekeeper, had explained to him that when the queen bee dies or stops producing, she must be replaced. Although it is easy enough to buy a new queen bee, if the beekeeper places her directly in the beehive, the other bees will react to her foreign scent and attack her until she dies.

To prevent this situation, beekeepers build a small wooden block about the size of a pack of cigarettes. The queen bee is placed in an inch-wide hole in the center of the block, which is then covered with two thin layers of porous material, thus protecting the bee while allowing air to pass through the hole. On one side of this wooden device, a small hole with a diameter of 4 millimeters is drilled all the way to the central hole, and is then filled with wax. Once the queen bee is placed inside, the rest of the bees try to attack her, but because the porous material protects her, they are unable to harm her. Some bees start to dig out the wax from the 4-millimeter-wide canal. In 90 percent of cases, by the time they get to the center, in a little over a week, the queen bee has taken on the scent of the rest of the colony, and they consequently take her as queen. In the remaining 10 percent of cases, the queen bee fails to adopt the scent of the rest of the colony and is killed by them.

When they fail to embrace the culture of their new hive, just like a queen bee keeping its strange scent, these brilliant executives do not become part of the team and are rejected by their colleagues, which can ultimately lead to failure and dismissal from the job. Whether it's the new queen, the new CEO, or a lower-level manager, when an individual does not behave according to the organizational culture, it will wake up a series of reactions from colleagues and end up in expulsion from the organization.

If one of the most powerful ways in which you shape a culture is through hiring and firing, then how does one identify candidates who share the values and behaviors that would make them successful additions to your organizational culture, and how do you ensure they will integrate smoothly into it? To begin with, if organizations want to be able to find candidates with similar values and effectively prepare new workers to take on that culture in a lasting and meaningful way, they must communicate and live by those elements every day. They must be clear about and embody that culture. If they do not, they will constantly grow a cemetery of queen bees. Likewise, if someone doesn't behave according to those values and behaviors in your organization, you need to fire him so that the rest of the people in the organization know that your values are for real, that they are committable, that you walk your talk. Clarity and consistency are key.

Because you want to hire people who naturally share the values and desired behaviors that make up your organizational culture, it is also crucial that both the hiring and firing processes include elements such as tests or questions that explore candidates' natural affinity and respect for the company's vision, values, trust, and strategic behaviors.

In an interview with Tony Hsieh, I asked him to tell me about the hiring process at Zappos.com. He told me that the company works with two sets of questions: first, the human resources sector asks questions about the candidates' competency for the vacant post; second, the other group of questions concentrates exclusively on the company's 10 core values. They are called "committable values" because the company is committed to them; it hires and fire people based on them, regardless of professional performance. Each of these criteria is assessed in every job interview and in every annual performance evaluation.

I was quite intrigued by this, so I asked, "Tony, one of those values is humility. How do you test a candidate with respect to that trait? Do you just ask, 'Sir, are you humble?'" He laughed and said, *"No, you're right. We don't ask that kind of question."* He went on:

> *When candidates arrive at our central offices, they take a shuttle from the parking lot to the main building, where they'll have their interviews. When they leave, we call the shuttle driver and ask him, "How did that candidate treat you? Was this person nice to you?" and if the person did not behave according to our values, we wouldn't hire him. We've rejected very important software programmers, which are really important for us, because they didn't have the human attitudes that we look for.*

Can you imagine an online retail giant rejecting an interested top-flight programmer because of how that programmer treated a shuttle driver? I hope, at this point in the book, you can. This seemingly simple example shows the extraordinary seriousness with which the world's most successful companies are now taking the role of culture. It can make or break careers—and companies. If a culture is respected and lived sincerely, at all costs, it is not a "nice to have" attitude, but rather the secret formula for extraordinary success.

The Key to Success? Firing Your Superstar!

This conversation with Hsieh brings me to another critical point, which I would sum up as, "What is the key to success? Firing your superstar!" Indeed, in Tony's opinion, a culture will pass the "acid test" when the company is ready to let go of an employee or manager who meets all of his quantitative objectives, but does not behave according to the company's values. When you are willing to do this, and only then, will people start believing that culture and values are something more than a plaque in the entrance hall or a document stuck in a drawer.

Jack Welch forcefully and explicitly states the same idea when it comes to firing people who meet the numbers but don't behave according to the cultural values:

> *Fire him and hang him at the public square! And don't say he left the company to spend more time with his family.*

Jack's system for employee performance evaluation relies on two dimensions: whether employees reach "the numbers" or not and if they live by the company's culture and values. Jack uses a chart whose x-axis represents conforming to company values, and whose y-axis stands for achieving quantitative "business" objectives—in other words, the numbers.

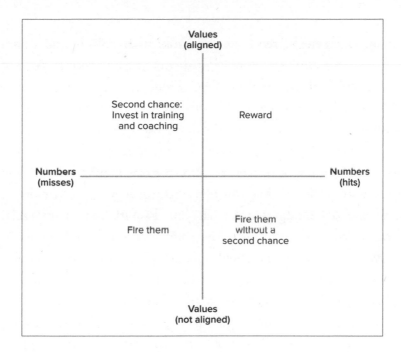

These criteria form four different quadrants that identify four different types of employees, ranging from first-rate to letdown. Evaluation is easy with the first two quadrants: on the one hand, those who fulfill both objectives are the first-rate employees who should be rewarded with bonuses, promotions, pats on the back, and other honors; on the other, those who neither get the numbers nor comply with the company's values should be fired.

The situation becomes a bit more complicated in the third quadrant, when people do not reach the numbers, but do live by the values. According to the General Electric human resources policies instituted during Jack's tenure, leaders should give these employees another chance because people who share the values and behaviors of the company can more easily upgrade their performance, which might have been hurt for incidental reasons; moreover, even if they don't necessarily improve their performance significantly, they don't undermine the culture, and it is important for management to reinforce the notion that culture and values are so important that embracing them may be more important than simply getting good numbers. Finally, the people in the last quadrant are those who reach their business objectives but do not conform to corporate values; those should be fired without a second chance, because if you keep those who don't have the values just because they bring you additional sales or juicy profits, you are shouting loudly that you don't believe in your own culture. Everyone is looking to see what you do with that commercial director who is great in surpassing sales goals but a total jerk when it comes to the values and behaviors that define your organization.

Remember that culture is what gives everyone a sense of purpose, pride, commitment, engagement, trust, and a sense of belonging. Would you imagine feeling all those strong, positive emotions when the top bosses keep a jerk who doesn't live up to the values and behaviors behind the culture, even if he has the numbers? If the bosses did that, they would be saying they value numbers more than people and culture. Clearly, I have labored to show how this is a losing strategy. Remember that culture exponentially multiplies results; one person with good numbers can't make up for that, so lose him. If you don't take these necessary steps, people will realize that your values are nothing but words that have no real effect, and they will stop believing in those guiding ideas. If you truly believe in the transformative power of an effective culture, you will be willing to fire even your "numbers superstar" to build trust and commitment in the rest of the team for that culture.

Monitoring Cultural Management: The Control Panel

Once a company incorporates elements of its culture into its performance evaluation systems and hiring and firing practices, it will really begin to manage its culture. If I, as a leader, do not measure the values and behaviors that I wish to see in my organization, it is unlikely that the members of the company will value and abide by them. On the other hand, if I measure and monitor them regularly, my employees will naturally start to live by these behavioral rules. Therefore, just as you would do with any important project, you must set up a *Leadership Control Panel*, which will be as necessary as an Income Statement or a KPI (Key Performance Indicators) Dashboard. You should choose between 5 and 10 values and strategic behaviors to form the core evaluation factors, but be cognizant of other necessary elements. Indeed, only if you identify and measure all the relevant issues and variables we have identified throughout the book—from the organization's purpose, values, and behaviors and developing the best in everyone to trust building and making sure you develop the appropriate communication and decision-making practices—will you be able to manage and strengthen your culture—and ultimately exploit its complete potential. I also recommend focusing more attention on high-ranking executives, and then moving on to middle management. If the people at the top of the structure live according to the culture, their subordinates will soon do the same.

In conclusion, the fifth role of a leader is defining, understanding, building, and managing your organizational culture. Establishing a culture plan is the key endeavor to the successful creation of a strong organizational culture. I hope that reviewing different types of culture—from purpose-driven to innovative—together with asking yourself key questions regarding your dreams, values, and behaviors has enabled you to better identify the elements of your own culture or to understand how you might plan a new one. I also hope that you understand the necessity of embedding the elements of your culture in all your traditional management systems—from recruiting to performance evaluation.

Only by using all available management tools, including a leadership control panel, will every member of the organization come to embody your culture and feel the fire that sparks everyone to enhance performance. For, remember, culture is about emotions. So, to check if you are leveraging this role of creating and managing culture, I invite you to ask yourself the following questions:

Are you proud, engaged, and happy?
Are your people, too?

CHAPTER 8

THE SKILLS AND TRAITS OF A CHIEF EMOTIONS OFFICER—CASE STUDY, POPE FRANCIS

How do you create companies that are as human as the people who work there?

—**Gary Hamel,** London Business School professor and director of the Management Innovation Exchange

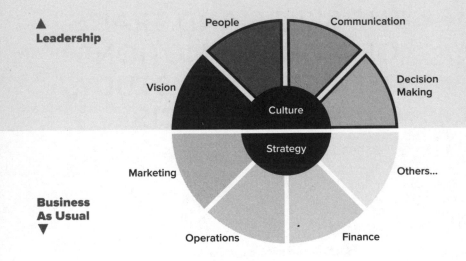

Leadership ▲

People

Communication

Vision

Decision Making

Culture

Strategy

Marketing

Others...

Business As Usual ▼

Operations

Finance

A FULLY INTEGRATED
MANAGEMENT MODEL

Now that we've seen the five key roles of the Chief Emotions Officer and how, when effectively employed, they foster the positive emotions and behaviors that enhance individual and team performance and help culture multiply results, it's important to ask what characteristics a person must have in order to successfully play the roles that make up the Chief Emotions Officer. We need to understand who you have to *be* or who you have to *become* in order to perform the actions involved in each role and fully realize the potential you have when you lead as the Chief Emotions Officer.

First, however, let's think back briefly to Chapter 2 and the graphic representation of the two halves that make up the fully rounded Chief Emotions Officer. I think we can now fully understand the dual framework.

The role of the Chief Emotions Officer is not only to take care of the business-as-usual, the hard variables, starting with a strategy, but to integrate that with the five key roles of a leader in order to fire up people's hearts and souls. The dual framework enables us to understand the key individual levers by identifying them, but we mustn't forget that they are all deeply intertwined and interrelated. Though culture's long-neglected status means that one should pay particular attention to the benefits of culture (and the emotional content so crucial to culture), strategy and culture are the twin engines with which the leader can drive the entire organization to success and its people to a higher fulfillment.

The question now is which skills and traits you need as a person to better fulfill those five roles, so in the following pages we will identify and analyze a number of the key traits, skills, and characteristics of great leaders. First, leaders must have certain attributes that pertain to how they deal with the world around them: a fundamental humanism, the humility to accept what they don't know, curiosity to explore the world, the willingness to learn continually, and the imagination and self-confidence to try new things. Second, they must also have certain skills related to how they treat people, particularly empathy and sensitivity. Third, a leader has to learn to deal with opposites with thoughtfulness, balance, and good judgment. Next, it warrants noting that most leaders look for the traits they themselves have in their team members. Finally, I uphold that you can develop your leadership skills by considering leadership as a personal and spiritual path. Indeed, I believe leaders should venture into this fantastic journey of improving their leadership traits by recognizing that it is a personal and spiritual path that requires authenticity and significant self-knowledge. You really change what you do when you change who you are.

THE GENERAL PERSONAL CHARACTERISTICS NEEDED

During my years of speaking with important businesspeople, I've frequently asked them about the key to their personal success in business—not how each of their respective companies became successful, but rather, which elements they saw as crucial in helping *them* reach *their* personal goals.

Empathy and Understanding: Be Humanistic

Although it might seem to fly in the face of conventional wisdom, one of the most common—and surprising—answers has been "my humanistic background." Herb Kelleher replied that way during an interview in his office at Southwest's Dallas headquarters. He told me a bit about his upbringing: *"My mom provided me with a humanistic background, and then I studied law, not business."* He believes that background and that education helped him to put people first:

> *My humanities background was very, very helpful . . . because it teaches you about the importance of human beings. If I had my way, I would make everybody get an arts degree before they got any other.*

Interestingly, one could argue that this personal trait played a significant role in Southwest's success, as it became the company's overarching value.

On a different occasion, as we walked through the park at his beautiful property in Malibu, Michael Eisner confessed: *"The key to my success is my humanist education."* Same words, same idea. As a young adult, Eisner abandoned premed studies in favor of English literature and theater and graduated from a small liberal arts college in Ohio with a BA in English. I find it interesting that the man who was among the greatest forces in the all-encompassing expansion of television and film as a mammoth business—earning himself hundreds of millions of dollars along the way—holds a liberal arts degree and credits those education principals with his enormous business and leadership success.

However, in my opinion, the story that best expresses the importance of a background in the humanities and how it gives one an advantageous humanist approach in the business world is that of A. G. Lafley. During his time as CEO of Procter & Gamble, P&G's market value doubled, making it one of the 10 most valuable brands in the world. One might assume that such a feat comes as a result of being deeply versed in the technics of business, business administration, and financial management, but Lafley pursued a liberal arts degree during his undergraduate career, focusing on history and literature. Only in his mid-30s did he decide it was time to go for an MBA.

Intrigued by this academic profile, I asked him which had been more valuable for him as a CEO: his training and degree in humanities or in business? Lafley let out a big laugh and said:

> *Frankly, as CEO, my liberal arts education and my broad educational background, including historical studies and everything from ancient history through the Renaissance, Russian history, [and] Asian history. MBA tools are practical; they serve you well when you are starting out; they help you learn the basics of business and, frankly, some of the key conceptual ways to think about an industry or a business. But you draw on your humanistic skills when you are leading people, and we had 135,000 people to lead inside P&G, and hundreds of thousands that were part of the P&G network.*

Although they claim to do many things to foster the professional development of their top executives, I do not personally know of any companies that take the time to train their executives in the humanities or liberal arts! Still, before addressing other personal and professional development concerns, all executives should acknowledge the importance of this "humanistic training" and pursue it. Leadership is about people and drawing them toward a common goal or dream. This requires understanding and, as we discussed in Chapter 2, empathy in particular. Because most aspects of leadership are strongly related to people, you need to be able to understand them deeply—understand their thoughts and moods, their needs and dreams. In order to apprehend how to coax someone into behaving in a certain way, you need to be able to feel what that person feels emotionally, putting yourself in that person's shoes. That is empathy, and it should be the priority in training for top management, particularly given the advent of globalization. As Carlos Ghosn points out in an article in consulting firm McKinsey & Company's quarterly journal: "Leaders of the future will also need to have a lot more empathy and sensitivity— not just for people from their own countries, but also for people from different countries and cultures. They are going to need global empathy, which is a lot more difficult."[1] The humanities and liberal arts are key in developing empathy and understanding. Subjects such as history, literature, philosophy, sociology, art history, and psychology enable you to better comprehend peoples' reasoning and motivations, and, in the end, to recognize and appreciate the immense complexity of human behavior.

Maybe that's also why the most innovative universities in the United States are beginning to show a preference for students with humanistic profiles in hopes of training students in this school of thought. Bestselling author on business and management Daniel Pink says that the Georgia Institute of Technology *"has a huge portion of its incoming freshmen who play a musical instrument"* Why? Because Georgia Tech is using that as a proxy for whole-mindedness. Pink insists:

> *They want people who are horizontal thinkers.*
> *They want people with a diverse set of interests;*
> *they want people who can communicate well.*

Why is Georgia Tech doing that?

Because employers are complaining. Employers are saying, "Don't send us this kind of narrow-minded, rule-based engineer. That kind of work we're sending overseas. Send us people who can think, who can juggle between the right and left brain, who have communication skills, who understand the business contact, who have a design sensibility."

I can attest to the fundamental importance of having a wide range of interests in preparing one to be a more successful and capable leader. In addition to my studies in engineering and business, I was a professional watercolor painter during high school and university, and it had a deep impact on the person I am today—particularly on how I see and approach the world. Being a watercolor painter taught me that things are not always the way they seem to be, that different lights can show different colors, that changing perspectives reveals different contours and different qualities in the same subject or environment. I am also passionate about dancing, from tango to rock and roll. This definitely has an impact on the way I look at people; it might have to do with seeing people move in a different way and seeing them relate to music differently than they relate otherwise. These interests have truly shaped me and play a role in everything I do—from negotiating to creating an entrepreneurial endeavor and hiring. I remember a conversation with a journalist from the German television company ZDF after an event at the impressive Alte Oper in Frankfurt. She said to me, "But you are a renaissance man!" This became the biggest compliment I have ever received!

Having a diverse set of interests and a humanistic background is important not only because of the advantages they give when dealing with people, but also because they are clear evidence of the desire to constantly learn.

Be Open to Constant Learning: The Importance of Curiosity, Imagination, and Humility

I need people that are curious, people that are imaginative. . . . I want people that anticipate—that see around the corner, the dangers and the opportunities.
—Colin Powell

Constant learning is an absolutely crucial characteristic for a successful leader because it includes three other important traits—curiosity, imagination, and humility.

Bill Conaty, who, as we explained earlier, was vice president of human resources at General Electric for almost 15 years, insists on the importance of constant learning when it comes to choosing new executives:

What we are looking for once someone is working for us is their capacity to continue learning. Is It someone who thinks they have the answer since the day they start? If it's like that, then we probably hired the wrong person. But we always look for individuals that want to constantly expand their minds, expand in a process of constant learning.

Why would the willingness to learn constantly be such an important quality that GE would have it as one of the implicit criteria for a good hire? Because, as Supervielle Financial Group CEO Patricio Supervielle says: *"Ultimately, leadership is the constant management of change."* As society and its expectations change, along with consumers' needs and the competition's way of addressing the market, a CEO must be able to react and change a company's strategy, as well as employees and their way of working, to meet new demands. Therefore, a CEO must participate in a process of constant learning so as to understand new developments, formulate an informed response, and make the necessary changes and adjustments. As Jack Welch insists, *"The capacity of an organization to learn and translate this learning quickly into actions is its most important competitive advantage."* Learning never ends. You can always learn from every situation in your daily life. Jack once explained, *"There is always somebody doing something that intrigues you. You learn from everybody."*

Nothing favors constant learning like curiosity. Although I wouldn't say that curiosity is a universal leadership personality trait, the majority of leaders that I've interviewed are just that—curious. Bestselling author and leadership expert Jim Collins finds the key to learning in curiosity: *"If there is something I'm proud of, it's my curiosity."* Curious people are open to the world and are naturally inclined to explore and understand it. This characteristic allows them to perform much better in different leadership tasks. For example, if you want to establish a vision, you must first understand the current context so that you can identify specific opportunities. You must also pay close attention to how the market and that context evolve, thus keeping yourself open to the possibility of modifying your dream or the general direction of the organization. A curious person is not only more likely to perceive these changes, but also to respond successfully to them by already being open to change. Plus, curious leaders are more capable of discovering and developing new talents in order to respond to change.

At the same time, curiosity is the trait that allows a person faced with a situation he doesn't fully understand to recognize that he doesn't know what to do, and then motivates him to go out and search for a solution. In this way, curiosity requires humility—in other words, acknowledging that you don't know or understand everything. As Rudy Giuliani says, *"You have to admit what you don't know."* But then you also have to feel the drive to go and look for an answer, which is why curiosity is intimately linked to the desire to continue to learn.

Famous soccer coach Miguel Angel Cappa described former footballer and current Bayern Munich coach Pep Guardiola as a *"very curious person who tries to absorb other people's experiences."*[2] Despite Guardiola's enormous achievement as a player—from the European Cup championship to an Olympic Gold medal—when this Spaniard was about to start his career as a coach, he traveled all around the world to interview the coaches he most respected and wanted to learn from. He had a huge desire to learn and wanted to cast his net as far and as wide as he could, understanding that learning can be found in any place and at any time and that even the most successful have something to learn, especially when they approach a new role.

I remember one particular manifestation of curiosity, a sincere lifelong desire to learn. Former United States secretary of state and U.S. ambassador to the United Nations Madeleine Albright had participated in a forum in Buenos Aires, my hometown. I had invited her to a special dinner with other speakers, but she was regrettably unable to accept because she was traveling back to the United States that same day. I accompanied her to the car that waited for her in the Convention Center's underground parking lot. Before she got in, I said: "Mrs. Albright, what a shame that you won't be able to stay for dinner tonight, because I was going to give one of my special tango lessons, and I was going to show you why tango is the most sensual dance in the world." As I've noted, I am passionate about dance and especially about tango. Wanting to share this as a special thanks to our speakers, I had prepared a special class for all of the international speakers. As soon as she heard those words, Madeleine Albright grabbed my arm, turned around, looked into my eyes, and said: *"Teach me now!"* And so, in the middle of that underground parking lot, as her assistant and chauffeur looked on, entertained, I taught the former secretary of state "the ABCs of tango."

The fact that a 70-year-old woman who had traveled all over the world and been to thousands of different places, met thousands of different people, and taken part in thousands of unique experiences was intrigued and curious enough to learn how to dance tango says a lot about her character—a character that keeps her connected to the world through a process of constant learning.

I would also argue that imagination is intimately linked to curiosity and constant learning. When I asked Francis Ford Coppola what were the key characteristics that made him so successful, he responded:

> *I have a very good imagination. For example, if we would have said, "We are not happy with the way the croissants are arranged on the dish," I would come up with 50 other ways to do it, so I think a very active imagination, and a lot of energy, and that is about it!*

Indeed, imagination is part of constantly searching for new answers to daily problems and issues. Colin Powell looks for people who are *"imaginative"* to be on his team, because he knows it takes imagination to be a problem solver. Rudy Giuliani sums it up like this: *"Be an optimist, a problem solver. Train yourself to think in solutions."*

Moreover, a leader must have imagination to look for new ways in which the world around us can be improved and to drive change. My meeting with Oscar-winning director, producer, and screenwriter James Cameron provides a perfect illustration of the way curiosity and the desire to learn come together with imagination, humility, and problem solving to change the very landscape of an industry for good. According to Cameron, he started working on the movie *Avatar* in 1994, almost 15 years before its release, but he had to put the project on hold for many years because he lacked the necessary technology to complete it. However, even once those technical resources became available, he faced an endless number of challenges that he could never have anticipated. That didn't stop him, though. It invigorated him. *"Guys, this is great!"* he explained. *"This is why I am making this movie. Because I want these moments where I don't know the answer, and you don't know the answer. So it was making the problem solving fun!"* In my view this quote shows several attributes: on one hand, it shows the willingness to accept that you might not have all the answers, a sign of humility, but, at the same time, it demonstrates curiosity and the drive for constant learning, for solving problems and having fun while doing so. How many of you would have the humility to tell your teams that you love those moments where nobody has the answer?

But apart from this, the most valuable thing that I learned from Cameron was during a conversation in which he shared one of the secrets to his success. I told him that I thought he was a great marketer, because he had been able to create three very different movies—*Terminator*, *Titanic*, and *Avatar*—all of which broke worldwide sales records. How did he know what people wanted? His response was a real learning moment for me: he believed that the key to his cinematographic success was that he created experiences that the viewer had previously been unable to imagine. How great is that! In Cameron's opinion, the key is to give the public more than they could ever dream of! To deliver that, you have to constantly look for new things—be curious to look outside the industry, to look for new technologies, to constantly learn. Indeed, that's what impressed me most about Cameron: like fellow innovative genius Steve Jobs, he created products that delivered experiences customers had not yet imagined; he was curious enough to dream up something as-of-yet unattainable and also had the imagination, problem-solving abilities, and self-confidence to continue to move forward.

Be Self-Confident

Although in Chapter 6 we spoke about the need for self-confidence in decision making, self-confidence is clearly a much broader, necessary trait. Self-confidence is a very powerful emotion for anyone who has the desire to change the world around him or her, and that is why it is intimately linked with problem solving and curiosity. As Clayton Christensen, professor of business administration at the Harvard Business School and author, says:

> *The curiosity to figure out why things happen the way they do and the confidence that you can fix things are attributes of successful innovators.*

Madeleine Albright echoed this idea. In an interview with her while Barack Obama was running for president of the United

States, I asked about the qualities most important to that office. She immediately said, *"Self-confidence and curiosity."*

Self-confidence is also necessary to those working for change because the changes you make rarely work the first time. You need to try over and over again, in one way, then in a different one. Self-confidence gives you the emotional energy to overcome failure by not blaming yourself, by not thinking that you are unable to achieve your goal. Self-confidence allows you to keep trying, to keep learning, to experiment, to problem solve, to innovate, and to make things in a new way.

Jack Welch agrees that self-confidence is the quality behind trying new things, learning from mistakes, and continuing to try:

> *Each time you feel self-confidence, you are willing to try new things as a leader. Some things don't work. But that is OK. I probably made more mistakes in business than anybody in business, because I tried more things, but I quickly learned from it.*

When Jack was a child, he used to stammer, and that was a big concern to him, especially considering his ambitions and the way people habitually treat those who stammer as lesser-abled. Jack believes that his mother, who constantly instilled in him a sense of self-confidence, is the reason behind his success—both in managing his stutter and in his long and illustrious career:

> *When I stammered, she told me: "Don't worry, Jack. Your tongue is not as fast as your brilliant mind."*

When others—particularly those you love and respect, like your parents—believe that you have all the capabilities to achieve anything you want, you will be gradually infused with enough self-confidence not just to keep trying new things, but to achieve more generally and continually. In fact, self-confidence builds every time we achieve something or we receive praise from someone we look up to. Jack calls this getting a *"shot of self-confidence."* The Chief Emotions Officer must have self-confidence, but she must also continuously build her team members' self-confidence by finding opportunities to give shots of self-confidence.

This ability to move forward through failure with self-confidence, trying new solutions to problems at the same time as you nurture your staff members' confidence, clearly requires a delicate balancing act, and that's why the ability to find balance and exercise good judgment is so necessary to the Chief Emotions Officer.

Be Able to Balance Multiple Traits and Practice Good Judgment

Sometimes people talk about the "visionary leader" who turns his back on his troops and marches forward. He concentrates solely on the role associated with his vision. But there's also the "orchestra conductor" who focuses on developing each individual's talent, helping people reach their full potential, and coordinating teamwork. The first case focuses on a leader who embodies the first leadership role, establishing a dream, whereas the second example represents a leader who is truly focused on caring for people, the second leadership role. Consider Steve Jobs in light of these. He was clearly a visionary leader with a tremendous ability to visualize what he wanted to create; however, as most of his close collaborators testify, he could treat people in a rather rough way. Jobs's ability as a visionary leader outstretched and had to compensate for his more difficult personal relationship skills—or lack of them. Other leaders may be very good at coordinating people and bringing out the best in each one—true orchestra conductors—but not entirely equipped to define a dream. Although many leaders are successful in one leadership role at the expense of another, the best leaders will be successful at multiple roles, even when these roles seem conflicting or diametrically opposed!

A leader must often embody—and ultimately learn to balance—opposite traits. Personally, I like the idea of opposites; it implies difference and may even mean that some of the leadership traits and skills that I've mentioned so far come into conflict. For example, a leader must be determined and perseverant so that he can insist on the path that he has chosen and not be intimidated or led astray by hurdles along the way. But, at the same time, he must be flexible enough to know when to change directions, when to stop, and when to modify his vision or the next milestone.

In this sense, the tension between nearly opposite characteristics can also help leaders grow. For example, you have to want to win with all your heart, but also learn to recognize defeat and move on to the next battle. You have to know when to listen to every person with something to say, but also when to stop and make your decision. And you must be able to figure out when to speed up and be persistent, and when to change. Yin and yang.

Indeed, in the end, it is about balancing, not opposing forces, but *complementary* forces. Learning balance as a leader is crucial, as Carly Fiorina insists:

> **Well, I think leaders have to strike the right balance. I like to say finding a balance is the core of leadership. The**

(continued)

> *right balance between so many things. The right balance*
> *between focus on execution and strategic vision. The*
> *right balance between [the] things . . . we have to keep*
> *the same and . . . [the] things must we change. The right*
> *balance between serving customers and empowering*
> *employees. All those are decisions about balance,*
> *you know? So, a leader, a good leader not only is not*
> *troubled by the ambiguity of balance, but understands*
> *that finding the right balance points is part of their job.*

Balance is the complex, rare trait of finding the fine equilibrium between very different options. To achieve that balance, a leader needs to have very good judgment. As A. G. Lafley said:

> **The CEO is the only one that can balance**
> **the investment in the future with the return**
> **of the present. It is a big judgment call.**

Having good judgment is what allows a good leader to make successful decisions when weighing different situations and opposing criteria. As we know, there are situations where the answer is "it depends." The thing that defines a strong leader is handling these situations with good judgment and knowing which of the opposing choices to make when the time comes: when to whole-heartedly insist on keeping a given direction and when to have the wisdom to change course, when to back up a stumbling business and when to shut it down. As a leader it's most important to learn how to balance different, even opposing, traits, while at the same time using good judgment as you strive to achieve different goals.

DEVELOPING THE TRAITS AND
SKILLS THAT DEFINE A LEADER

Thus far this chapter, we have focused on the characteristics a leader must have. Leaders are humanistic, understanding, and empathetic problem solvers with vast imagination, intelligence, curiosity, good judgment, and the self-confidence to follow their hearts and, if necessary, go against the grain. OK, but what do you do once you've identified these traits and skills? Take a good, hard look at yourself and ask honestly, "Do I have these skills already, or do I need to develop them? Do these characteristics already make up who I am, or am I going to have learn them fresh?"

It certainly helps if you've been brought up in an environment that has fostered the personality characteristics and skills you need for leadership. In fact, I am convinced that leaders are forged during their first 18 years of life, meaning that family education and culture is where future leaders develop most of the necessary characteristics. Welch, Branson, and Bill Clinton, among other great leaders, have special relationships with their mothers. Remember Clinton saying his mother was his mentor? Earlier in this chapter, we heard Jack mention the crucial role his mother played in his life. My grandmother's father was Jose Luis Cantilo, a lawyer, journalist, and politician who not only founded a national newspaper and several journals, but was also governor of the Province of Buenos Aires, mayor of the City of Buenos Aires, a member of Congress and speaker of the house, and a member of the National Academy of History. He bequeathed a legacy of humanism, inquiry, and empathy that has pervaded my family ever since. My father once told me he believes that this family history and the culture it created have a lot to do with my achievements not as a businessman, but as an interviewer and intellectual.

Regardless, know that you can learn or improve on the traits and skills that define a leader! Developing them is a conscious job, and there's always interior work to be done. That's why I would invite you to grab a blank sheet of paper and write down what you want to do in your role as leader. Consider these questions:

- What dream do I want to achieve at the head of my organization or team?

- Do I care about my group's well-being?

- Do people communicate effectively and fluidly throughout my company?

- Do my team members have the elements they need to reach their fullest potential?

- Am I proud and happy to belong to this team?

Next, write down the characteristics or skills that you want to develop, and try to do something each day to get better at them. For example, how can you be more curious? One way you could address this is by googling something entirely new to you each day. Or, sit down for coffee once a week with your team and ask each person to talk for five minutes about something he or she learned that week. You have to train yourself to be curious, and it's addictive!

Similarly, you can practice being more focused on people, being more straightforward, or being more courageous. When you are able to understand and feel who you are and what you want, you will see many more leadership characteristics of other leaders emerge within you.

Finally, I invite you to draw a development plan based on where you are right now and where you want to be by the end of the year. Make a summary, reflect on it, talk about it with others, and write about it. Most of all, practice the skills that will get you there!

Be Authentic

This practice will be a big step; however, developing these skills will not be enough. I think that this is the first "bad news" in this whole book. As you practice these skills, you will learn how to perform them properly. But the foundation of all leadership isn't what you do or say, but what you choose to be. And you can't fake that. It just doesn't work. I insist that it's not just about imitating others' actions or learning the skills created and practiced by others. At the end of the day, everyone knows whether what you're doing is a true reflection of who you are. Of course, doing certain things will eventually help you change who you are, but you need to be willing to be transformed. So, in order to be a true leader, you must grow internally and make those actions an authentic reflection of who you really are. Be authentic. Be yourself.

Indeed, the starting point for growth, the starting point on the long path toward effective leadership, is always authenticity. It doesn't matter where you are, start with that! Once more, Welch says it wonderfully, full of passion:

> *Be authentic! Authenticity is one of your greatest attributes. Whoever the hell you are, be that person. Don't end up trying to look like somebody else, act like somebody else, be somebody else. Be yourself. Be comfortable in your own shoes. It will end up being probably the most important thing you do.*

Christie Hefner would certainly agree with Welch's sentiment:

> *But in one sense I think I am very much like my father [Playboy founder Hugh Hefner] in that I really do believe you have to be true to yourself, so my father lives his life not because he thinks it's good promotion for the company. He lives his life because he thinks that makes him happy.*

LEADERSHIP AS A PERSONAL AND SPIRITUAL PATH: GET TO KNOW YOURSELF

You can only lead others if you lead yourself.
—**Alex Rovira,** author and business consultant

This call to authenticity begs the question: if authenticity is the starting point on the long path toward effective leadership and growth, then in order to be authentically myself, must I not know who I am? Yes! That's why I firmly believe that developing as a leader is a process that also requires growing as a person—and the first step in growing as a person is actually getting to know yourself. Indeed, the first thing you need to do is realize that leadership—particularly the path of the Chief Emotions Officer—is a personal and spiritual journey of growth.

Therefore, the final key to leadership is to set out on a path toward self-discovery. For "Get to know yourself," we could also say, "Lead yourself!" or, even better, paraphrasing the Second Commandment, "Lead others as you would like to be led!" As

Bill George, former CEO of Medtronic, professor of management practice at Harvard Business School, and author, insists,

> *In my studies of hundreds of leaders that have failed, none of them have failed to lead other people. They have failed to lead themselves.*

You have to understand who you are, what your talents are, what you want, and how you want to live out your professional or entrepreneurial calling. I said the same thing when I discussed finding my own vision or dream, and one might understand this self-discovery as finding a vision for yourself, a dream of your future self. You have to ask: Why am I here on earth? How do I want to change the world?

Of course, these are not questions that you answer once and for all, but quests that you undertake over many years. Nevertheless, when you start to figure out that *why* and *how*, you become totally connected with your talents and your passions; you significantly increase your capacity to act. When you approach this journey with passion, you will find that you really can change your reality and the world around you.

Let me explain this by turning to my own personal history. At one point, many of my interviews and conversations were colored by my own midlife crisis, a crisis that had to do with challenging and breaking with external mandates, being able to find what I really liked, and pursuing it relentlessly in all aspects of life. I was in my early forties, in a crisis in my marriage, but passionate about my job. I was convinced that with one question you could easily spot those who were before a midlife crisis, those who were in it, and those who were after it. That question was, "Do you know your passions in life?" People before their crisis may know their obligations and perhaps even what they like or enjoy. A passion, though, is something altogether different. It goes well beyond simply enjoying something. When you are passionate, you forget lunch or any meal because you are engulfed in, completely taken by, what you are doing; you have an amazing amount of energy to do what you love. When you don't know your passions, you just do what you have to do, and that leads to an empty life.

So how do you find your passion? A lot of it is, of course, serendipity. When I started interacting with the speakers we engaged, I quickly, though quite surprisingly, discovered a real passion for interviews—a passion that has become the dream I live to this day, even when others have fallen away.

The famous filmmaker and entrepreneur George Lucas arrived at his passion and talent in a similarly serendipitous manner. In a conversation we had, I learned that Lucas didn't know that his passion was filmmaking. *"I never really paid attention to movies,"* he told me. *"I went to movie theaters to chase the girls, not to watch the movies."* It wasn't until he was at Modesto Junior College studying social sciences—he was interested in photography and art, but his parents refused to pay for it—that he took his first production class, a course in animation. He recalls:

[W]ithin two months, they've given me a camera test—so, how you operate a camera, all the things you have to do, move in, pull back. And I took that little test, which was less than a minute long, and I turned it into a movie. And that movie went on to win all kinds of awards all over the world, and I realized, "I know how to do this." I just was very good at it, and I loved it, and that's when I fell in love with movies and I found my passion.

Lucas and I both had the luck to stumble upon our passions, to learn almost by accident what we truly, passionately loved to do. But there's no need for you to rely upon luck. You can discover your passion through a spiritual journey, a quest to get to know yourself and what truly makes you happy, what serves as the fundamental guiding purpose of your life. Lucas offers great guidance on how to start this process:

> *When you ask yourself "What am I good at?," a good test is "What I enjoy doing." What is it, when you sit down and you don't have anything to do, what would you like to spend your time doing? And that usually is what you will have a passion for.*

Leaders like Lucas excel in what they do because they find what their passions are and they pursue them. Their personal passion then works as their own internal dream, as what leads them in their own life. Yes, passion gives purpose, and purpose acts like a constant motivator. It pulls all your resources from within; it takes the best out of you because you want to achieve that purpose. As such, passion is also a significant element on the road to happiness—to *achieving* happiness. Living your passion, exercising your talents toward an intensely believed purpose, and making a difference in this world—doing what you *wish*, in the full-fledged meaning of the term—are major components of happiness. And it is that absolutely personal definition of happiness that will drive your life by feeding your passion. Indeed, passion is the emotion that lies at the intersection of what you deeply enjoy, your talents, and your purpose. Passion is the "acid test" that allows you to enact your maximum leadership potential, giving you an amazing amount of energy to execute, to overcome obstacles, to bring people together, and, most important, to change things. Without it, you just plod along unfeelingly doing your duty and accepting the world as it is—a follower, not a leader.

Think about it. Your ultimate role as the New CEO is to be the Chief *Emotions* Officer; each of the five major roles you play has, at its heart, the production of emotion. No other emotion drives one as much as or in the way that passion does. That is the reason why each time I met with a leader—on stage at an event or in an intimate meeting at another time—I asked the same question over and over: "What is your passion in life?" Passion is at the foundation of everything a good leader does and everything a good leader is. You need to understand—in everyday situations and in crises—what you're most passionate about and what you will do to attain or protect it. You need to know what will drive you emotionally to achieve beyond the status quo. You need to probe what things will push you to change your reality and those around you and to meet goals you may as yet not even be able to imagine.

Here are a few of the answers I received from some of the world's most compelling leaders—answers from people who know what they want in life and go after it passionately, which is ultimately the best foundation for becoming a good leader. With each one of their answers, you understand why they lead in their fields. I would encourage you to read and consider these responses and to then ask yourself that question. It can be good to jump-start your personal journey.

> *My passions have to do with being able to make a difference, and I don't want this to sound naive, but it took me a very long time as a woman of a certain age to develop an independent voice, and to be able to make clear what I cared about, which has a lot to do with*

*social justice, with poverty, with women's rights, human
rights in general, the rule of law. And I felt that having
found my voice I wouldn't shut up. So my passion is
using whatever I have been able to acquire in terms of
personality and voice in order to make a difference.*
—**Madeleine Albright**

*I believe, you know, because in any profession, all of us
want to make some kind of difference. But I think the
challenge is, whatever you're doing, you have to commit
yourself to a problem that looks almost impossible, much
bigger than you are—you have no right to even think
you're going to change it. But if you have the guts to do
that, you wake up every morning knowing you have to
do more, you have to figure some way of sort of tackling
this, you need a different approach. . . . So that's what's
driving me at the moment: how do you create companies
that are as human as the people who work there.*
—**Gary Hamel,** London Business School professor and
director of the Management Innovation Exchange

My passion is people. . . . My passion is curiosity.
—**Herb Kelleher**

*My definition of success in life is that when you are
about to die, and you sit there—hopefully in the bed,
but wherever you are, lying in the trench or wherever
you are going to die—and you think, "When I die,
I did everything I wish, so I can die very happy."
You—I know—you have six kids! You are a lucky
man. You are actually the richest man I know!*
—**Francis Ford Coppola**

POPE FRANCIS

Yes, your passion, dream, and vision can change reality. A leader is the person who has the passion to change reality and the awareness that he can do it, regardless of how ambitious that change is. Once you have that awareness, you will go from being a victim of change to a protagonist. In the end, leadership comes down to being an agent of change—whether it's shifting market strategy and vision or radically altering hundreds of years of social and cultural practice.

Indeed, great leaders arise when there are big issues to be changed. When the world calls for significant change, leaders take responsibility for those changes on their shoulders. Of all the modern leaders that I have had the chance to speak with, I would choose Pope Francis, the first pope from the Americas, as the example of the new leadership exemplified by the figure of the Chief Emotions Officer. Not only does he exemplify each of the five roles I have sketched over the course of this book, sparking emotions in believers and nonbelievers alike with everything from his new vision for the church to his decisions and the way he communicates with the world; he also has all of the characteristics that we've just discussed—a genuine care for humanity, empathy, understanding, sensitivity, and the self-knowledge of a rigorous personal and spiritual journey. Furthermore, he has also put on his shoulders the tremendous duty of changing an organization that has played a crucial role in the world for nearly 2,000 years, and he has pursued this goal with the passion fitting his office. He seems to keenly realize that passion sparks change because it touches peoples' emotions—an idea at the heart of the Chief Emotions Officer concept. So, whether or not one agrees with the Catholic institution in general or finds my choice of Pope Francis as the ultimate example through which to demonstrate the tenets of the Chief Emotions Officer a somewhat intriguing and potentially peculiar choice, it's important to highlight that we'll analyze Pope Francis—named Man of the Year 2013 by *Time* magazine—from the point of view of leadership and through the looking glass of the leadership roles, and I hope it will be clear to you why he is a fitting choice to close this book. Let's take a look at the awe-inspiring passion that has created this unique leader.

Pope Francis is revolutionizing one of the most traditional institutions in the world, the Catholic Church. If someone had asked me which organization would be the most difficult to lead and change in terms of its culture, I would have immediately thought of the Catholic Church, an institution with over 1.2 billion members and an overwhelmingly horizontal structure for an organization of its size. Indeed, there are only three levels: one pope, 5,150 bishops, and 415,000 priests serving 1.2 billon Catholics worldwide! Moreover, there are 2,000 years of tremendous, tumultuous history—a history that has produced one of the most profound and unyielding cultures ever to have existed. Leading such a huge and complex organization is probably one of the most difficult leadership challenges I can think of, so, the differences between a business and a church notwithstanding, it may in fact be the best case study in which to explore what I have proposed throughout this book.

In his three years as pope, Jorge Bergoglio, now Francis, has had a massive impact on the whole organization and continues to make even more momentous changes to both the church and the greater world. He has decided to play a role and have a voice in numerous major global issues that technically go beyond the church itself, from peace between Palestine and Israel to climate change and sustainability issues, from immigration policy in Europe to the global economic system. On each one of these topics, Pope Francis has taken a strong position that is geared toward changing reality. Additionally, he has launched ambitious initiatives for reform within the Catholic Church. From a management dimension, he is working on reforming the Vatican Curia and decentralizing the church, giving significant power back to the Episcopal Commissions over the decisions that have to do with their own daily life. Never we have seen a pope who insists so much that he is the simply the "Bishop of Rome," in a clear reference to the need for the decentralization of decisions. On a more doctrinal dimension, he has decided to acknowledge and talk about touchy issues like the remarriage of divorced persons, homosexuality, abortion, the priesthood of married men and celibacy, and the role of women in the church.

Informing each of these engagements—these actions or behaviors—is indeed a series of values and a passionate dream for the Catholic Church and the world. Pope Francis aims to touch lives, to spark emotions and change reality by the recreation of a culture. This is the aim of the new leader, and reading what Pope Francis has done thus far through the prism of the Chief Emotions Officer's five roles enables us to understand how he has done it and why he has had such a deep impact.

A Dream: A Poor Church for the Poor

Since the moment he was elected pope, and even before appearing in public for the first time, then-Cardinal Bergoglio made the most important decision of his papacy, sending a powerful message to his immense audience. By choosing the name *Francis* in honor of Saint Francis of Assisi, the pope laid out his vision and dream for the church: to transform it again into a poor church for the poor.

Saint Francis lived in the early thirteenth century, and due to his concern about poverty and care for the poor, has represented through the centuries the claim for the church hierarchy to remain humble and poor, true to the message of Jesus. Because this quest is undoubtedly very difficult, particularly given the history of the Catholic Church, no bishop had ever—until now—had the courage to name himself Francis when becoming a pope. The choice of Pope *Francis* was a clear signal of the new pontiff's vision for the church as one in which the institution is close to the people and its problems, rather than cut off and above them. He has said: "I ask myself: What are the reasons—inside the church—why the worshipers aren't feeling satisfied? It's the lack of closeness. Today Catholics are called to be close, to go out and get near the people, their problems, their realities." It is this radical and ambitious vision that has shaken and now shapes the whole organization. For instance, in June 2015, Pope Francis presented part of his vision in the form of a bold 184-page papal encyclical that focused on the effects of climate change—particularly in terms of its effects on the world's poor and on escalating poverty—and called for immediate, far-reaching global action.

People: He Genuinely Cares for Each One

In a conversation I had with Pope Francis, he talked about his vision for a reborn church, meeting the people, connecting with them, caring about them. ***"On every occasion,"*** he told me, ***"I go to meet the people."*** He cares for people and is genuinely interested in them; he is moved by them. From the very beginning of his papacy, Francis has used small gestures to demonstrate the intimate, human approach that he wants to see in the church. He looks at each person when he is walking through the crowd, and he continues calling his friends in Buenos Aires when he hears that they are having a problem. In fact, he breaks all protocols to get into people's hearts. He personally called a young man in Granada, Spain, who had allegedly been abused by a priest, to ensure him of the church's full support in finding the truth and having the culprits assume responsibility.

As I said previously, Pope Francis argues that the church and its doctrine should be in the service of the people. In his view, the church today needs the capacity to cure the wounds of the people, to care for them, and to give "warmth to their hearts" by being close to them. "I see the church as a field hospital after the battle," he says, emphasizing the role of the church in taking care of people. One manner of realizing this belief was his first trip as pope, which was to Lampedusa, the small Italian island in the Mediterranean very close to Libya. Thousands of African emigrants strive to reach Lampedusa in order to get a new life in Italy and Europe, but many die in the sea crossing. For all of them, Lampedusa represents the tragedy of and hope for all African people in despair. Going to a small island that represents suffering and that shelters those who are suffering to actually meet the suffering people in person—to look them in the eyes and shake their hands—shows both a consistency with his vision—a church that takes care of the poor—and a deep personal approach and caring: he could have signed a special aid bill sitting in Rome, but he did not. To have made this his first trip as pope suggests the commitment he has to people, that he cares about them, and that he is determined to take care of them.[3]

Communication: The Power of Example

If his chosen name as pope represents his vision—the synthesis of what he wants to achieve in the church during his papacy—then his daily behaviors communicate it with a simple, coherent, and consistent attitude: he really walks the talk. For instance, in terms of attire, he prefers to use his personal wooden cross instead of a gold one and old black shoes instead of the traditional elegant red ones. Furthermore, ever since his days as a bishop in Buenos Aires, Pope Francis has lived in austerity, taking public transportation in the city and refusing any type of luxury, including those provided to him because of his important position. Even the same day that he was appointed as pope, the pontiff got on a bus with all of the cardinals who had chosen him, despite having a private limousine available. He denied those comforts to affirm his real and sincere message with actions, the same message that he preaches to thousands of churchgoers every day: simplicity and austerity.

Francis is an excellent communicator and devoted to reaching as many people as he can. Like every leader of his stature, he has a Twitter account with a daily tweet. But, more, he is afraid neither to overtly address difficult topics with his community and those beyond it nor to address and take responsibility for mistakes of the organization. In addition to very publically taking on climate change and its significant economic effects throughout the world in his papal encyclical, he encourages an open and public debate about controversial topics such as homosexuality, divorce, priestly celibacy, and abortion. These subjects have been taboo for centuries in the church but are now being addressed with candor and humility in almost every press conference. By addressing the issues and responding to the questions the community has, Pope Francis has become closer to the people's concerns and reality. By talking about them, he demonstrates that he knows how to listen, is empathetic, and recognizes the needs of his community. He has publically apologized and asked for forgiveness for the sexual scandals that church members have been involved in, a clear example of humility, straightforwardness, and respect for his parishioners, in addition to pursuing legal action against those implicated. Addressing the issues hasn't solved them all, but it creates a connection with the members of the community and is key in building trust.

Decision Making: Toward a More Open and Transparent Church

Effective decision making requires empowerment and strong-handed decisions that reflect *your own* decision. Pope Francis leverages controversy to exemplify the personal values that lie behind each decision and define each of his behaviors—and those he wishes to see from his followers. He really is someone who makes his own decisions. In attempting both to change the vision of the church and to align it with what he wants as a leader, Pope Francis has had to make his own decisions, even when those decisions go against history and the advice or opinions of some of his advisors and constituents. As we have seen, a true leader creates a vision, enacts it in example, and makes decisions in line with it and in order to accomplish it even if those decisions are unpopular or against the advice and opinion of both advisors and constituents.

In an unprecedented and controversial decision, completely illustrative of the change that he seeks to generate in the church, Pope Francis decided to baptize the baby of a couple who had not been married in the church and promised a single mother that he would baptize her child if she was unable to find any other priest willing to do it. These decisions are his decisions, and they express the value of being close to and caring about the poor. As such, they align practice with the vision. Moreover, with these decisions and his example, Pope Francis rocked the ecclesiastical hierarchy and the part of its constituents who do not agree with breaking the rules—which includes some of his advisors—at the same time as he modeled the appropriate behavior for the entire church.

With decisions and actions such as these, the Holy Father made clear what he expects of all members of the institution: a much more open and receptive attitude toward parishioners. In his opinion, the church cannot "control" the grace of God, but rather must "dispense" it to all those who want to get closer to God through the institution.

Perhaps one of the most significant decisions Pope Francis has made to date actually concerns the decision-making system itself and, not surprisingly, was among one of the first decisions he made. Even before he ascended to the papacy, Jorge Bergoglio clearly understood the history of deeply embedded corruption plaguing the Vatican bureaucracy—the kind that gave rise, not even two years before, to the Vigano Scandal, where the Governatorato, the organization that manages a significant portfolio of real estate in the Vatican, worked systematically with the same suppliers, with no public call for offers, and with prices that doubled market levels and therefore lined the pockets of a select few. It was very clear in the mind of the new pope that he needed to cut off the rotten part of the apparatus, so, in order to do this, he had to build a new team outside of the old, staunchly corrupt system to advise and inform him as he governed the church and prepared a plan for revising the Apostolic Constitution on the Roman Curia. A month after his election to the papacy, he created the "G8," a counseling board composed of eight cardinals, to help him govern the church and, in particular, reform the Roman Curia, especially in terms of corruption and mismanagement. These cardinals come one from each continent, one from the Roman Curia, and one coordinator from Latin America. The choice of people with different backgrounds and ideologies confirms both that he looks for people who can challenge him in good faith and that he has created a decision-making structure that allows him access to information and expertise that may be beyond his own.

That said, as many of the examples I have already given attest, this is not a situation that requires consensus. Pope Francis undoubtedly hears his advisors' advice and opinions, but he just as unmistakably makes his own decisions. For instance, in July 2013, five months into his papacy and only three short months after the formation of the G8, Pope Francis signed several *motu proprio*—decrees expressly based on his own decision and personally signed by him—reforming the Vatican's Criminal and Administrative Law to harden the sentences against sexual abuse and offenses entailing corruption and money laundering and creating several commissions to evaluate and control the Vatican finances.

Simply put, Pope Francis has made his own decision to forge a new organizational culture.

Culture: A Church for the Poor, a Church That Is Close to Everyone

With more than 13 million followers on Twitter and over 1.25 billion Catholics across the globe, Francis is one of the most influential public figures in the world. And although it may sound rather difficult with such a large and widespread organization to create the sort of unified set of values and behaviors that we've discussed as necessary for a strong organizational culture, Pope Francis has arguably been more successful at actively accomplishing this than many of his predecessors. He has sought to modernize the Catholic Church by establishing an inclusive and current culture that can create a greater bond with more people, thus allowing the institution to enjoy the shine and influence of past eras, and with his actions and a clear desire to communicate openly, he has already played an extremely important role in the church's rebirth: the number of people that attend mass has increased all around the world; there are plans to carry out deep reforms, such as promoting a more transparent management of church financial statements; in his search for a way to "healthily decentralize" the church, he has increased laypersons' responsibilities and given women and young people a more important role, all with the goal of modernizing the institution to respond to present-day needs and expectations; there is even a plan for establishing an "open-door culture" so that those who want to be close to the church won't find the "coldness of closed doors" and countless other obstacles to practicing their faith.

But more than anything, Pope Francis's dream and the culture he has wished to create for the church is a church for the poor. The values and behaviors he has set out to guide this unique organizational culture are being close to the people and in their service, simplicity and austerity so that the church can move more toward the poor, and candor and consistent communication to enable a heated discussion of the uncomfortable topics that touch the everyday lives of the people. These values and behaviors have then had to be embedded in the new culture as though through a "culture plan" and ultimately managed.

To take just one example of how a guiding value of the culture plays out and manifests itself in the behavior of everyone in the organization, starting at the top, let's look briefly at austerity. It is said that, during the first months when he finished up late, Pope Francis would walk through the empty offices turning off the lights to save energy.[4] He also eliminated the extra bonus that the 3,000 Vatican employees would normally receive when there is a change in pope to compensate for the extra work and effort. In 2005, for instance, with the death of John Paul II, they had each received 1,000 euros, plus 500 euros for the election of Benedictus XVI. In contrast, Francis decided to give that money—approximately 6 million euros—to charity.[5] This is not to mention the

Mercedes-Benz limousine that has given way to the small, middle-class car that is the Ford Focus!

It's clear how the organizational culture's expression starts with the values and behavior of the one at the top walking the talk, but what about the rest of the organization? Well, to begin with, Pope Francis has expressly vowed that the first criterion for naming bishops is that they are shepherds "close to the people." Simultaneously, he has removed the clerical officials who lived in luxury, who were obsessed with their own power, and who remained closed within the Vatican walls, far away from the people and their problems. That was the fate of the powerful secretary of state, Tarcisio Bertone. Five months into his job, Pope Francis fired him and replaced him with Pietro Parolin, not only the youngest in the job since the early twentieth century, but also a person that is foreign to the core of the Vatican cohort that has been in power for the last few decades. The values of being close to and caring for the people and embracing austerity and simplicity are therefore impacting the hiring and firing—two things key to creating a strong culture.

In Conclusion: A Deeply Personal Culture in Leadership

Although it is certainly not an easy task to start and carry out the reforms Pope Francis has proposed for a 2,000-year-old organization with one of the most profound and complicated histories and deeply embedded cultures imaginable, Francis is a leader who exemplifies coherently and effectively the five roles proposed in this book. He proposed a dream of having a poor church to service the poor; he then goes beyond all the protocol barriers to show that he cares for the people, that he understands their expectations and sufferings. He communicates relentlessly to establish a connection with worshipers, to build trust, to address all the issues that have been taboo. Ultimately, to make an effective change, he needs to empower the church around the world. So he insists on what the vision is, setting the differentiating values and behaviors to conform to a new culture, one in which the hierarchy is closer to the people. In the end, Pope Francis wants to touch lives—to change lives, to change reality—and he rallies his emotions and those of his followers in the service of this dream. Pope Francis's leadership, just like the cultural change that he is implementing, is inspired by one of the greatest leaders of all times, Jesus of Nazareth, who mastered the five leadership roles.

In my conversation with Pope Francis, I was amazed to hear how so much of what he said jibed with the leadership roles we have discussed in this book and the traits one needs to execute them well. I asked him about the key behind his leadership, and the first thing he answered, with a very big smile on his face, was:

"I don't know yet! I don't have the secret . . ."

At first this answer deeply surprised me, but then I thought more about it and thought more about our conversation, where he explained how each occasion is a discovery of the other, of his or her needs. Not having a secret means that Pope Francis genuinely does what he thinks is the right thing to do at each crossroads, and each one of these decisions and actions is the result of a lifetime of experience and meeting with and caring for people. In my view, his answer shows that great leaders don't have a "to-do list" or follow a recipe, and great leaders don't always conceptualize what they do. They just do it! They have grown to be leaders, not just learned to imitate the actions of great leaders. They have it inside. Whatever they do is the result of many years of learning to be themselves. Pope Francis's first thought when he was named pope by his fellow Cardinals was *"Jorge, don't change; continue to be you."*[6]

Pope Francis's example serves to give us a wonderful look at the origins of leadership as the Chief Emotions Officer and the way that organizational and personal culture meet in this kind of leadership. Great leadership starts with discovering your personal dream or vision and nurturing your own personal values in order to develop the foundations of an organizational culture. When you know what impact you want to make in the world, you either create that organization and recruit people who share your vision and values or you identify an existing organization and you join it. It's a journey that starts personal and grows to encompass the organization you lead or participate in: learn who you are and what you want to be, then find the organizational culture you want that jibes with who you are and your vision. Once you do, you will be fired up with a sense of purpose and the passion to change the world. Bring your personal values, your personal culture, your individual passion, and use it in the service of that organizational culture and its dream. When you do, you will fire up those around you.

Throughout this book, I have tried to extract the lessons and wisdom I've gleaned through over a decade's worth of conversations with some of the most successful, thoughtful, and interesting leaders of the twentieth and twenty-first centuries in order to share them with you in your quest to become a better leader, the Chief Emotions Officer. I hope you were able to learn from it. Of course, how you weave in the different roles and suggestions depends on who you are and the constantly changing context, but I am convinced that the essence of leadership remains the same: the CEO for the future is an agent of change with the passion to drive toward a dream while caring for the people in the organization and awakening the positive emotions that enable them to achieve true success individually and as a group.

We are all invited to that journey! So jump-start it right now!

Notes

Prologue

1. See https://en.wikipedia.org/wiki/Jack_Welch. See also http://
www.businessweek.com/1998/23/b3581001.htm: "So giddy are
some Wall Street analysts at GE's prospects that they believe that
when Welch leaves at the end of the year 2000, GE's stock could
trade at $150 to $200 a share, up from $82 now, and the company
could be worth $490 billion to $650 billion. 'This guy's legacy will
be to create more shareholder value on the face of the planet than
ever—forever,' says Nicholas P. Heymann, a onetime GE auditor
who follows the company for Prudential Securities."

2. According to https://en.wikipedia.org/wiki/Frederick_Winslow_
Taylor, "Taylor's scientific management consisted of four
principles: Replace rule-of-thumb work methods with methods
based on a scientific study of the tasks. Scientifically select, train,
and develop each employee rather than passively leaving them to
train themselves. Provide 'Detailed instruction and supervision
of each worker in the performance of that worker's discrete task'
(Montgomery 1997: 250). Divide work nearly equally between
managers and workers, so that the managers apply scientific
management principles to planning the work and the workers
actually perform the tasks."

3. https://en.wikipedia.org/wiki/Strategy.

4. https://en.wikipedia.org/wiki/Peter_Drucker#cite_ref38.
5. https://www.youtube.com/watch?v=vJG698U2Mvo.
6. http://www.forbes.com/sites/joshbersin/2015/03/13/culture-why-its -the-hottest-topic-in-business-today/.

Chapter 1

1. This was the definition of pornography put forth by Supreme Court Justice Potter Stewart in 1964. Later cases framed the very strict standards that the Supreme Court uses today.
2. *Merriam-Webster's Learner's Dictionary*, http://www.merriam -webster.com/dictionary/culture.
3. The exception to this is when there is an acquisition. In that case the price in excess of the total amount of assets has to be added to the Balance Sheet as an asset under various names (Brand, Goodwill, etc.).
4. http://www.greatplacetowork.com/our-approach/what-are-the -benefits-great-workplaces.
5. John P. Kotter and James L. Heskett, *Corporate Culture and Performance* (New York: Free Press, 1992).
6. Tony Schwartz, "Companies That Practice 'Conscious Capitalism' Perform 10x Better," *Harvard Business Review*, April 4, 2013.
7. Quote from David F. Bartlett, research director at Ladenburg, Thalmann & Co., in Bill Sing, "GE in Negotiations to Acquire 80% of Kidder, Peabody," *Los Angeles Times*, April 25, 1986.
8. https://en.wikipedia.org/wiki/Kidder,_Peabody_%26_Co.
9. https://en.wikipedia.org/wiki/Jack_Welch. "Through the 1980s, Welch sought to streamline GE. In 1981 he made a speech in New York City called 'Growing fast in a slow-growth economy.' Under Welch's leadership, GE increased market value from $12 billion in 1981 to $280 billion, making 600 acquisitions while shifting into emerging markets." See also http://www.cnbc.com/2014/04/29/25 -jack-welch.html.
10. *Money* magazine revealed that, during the 30-year period 1972– 2002, Southwest produced the highest return to shareholders of any company included in the S&P 500 during that 30-year period. http://swamedia.com/channels/Officer-Biographies/pages/ herb_kelleher.
11. Lou Gerstner, *Who Says Elephants Can't Dance?* (New York: HarperCollins, 2002).

Chapter 2

1. A summary of the definitions provided by *The Free Dictionary* (www.thefreedictionary.com), *Merriam-Webster Dictionary* (www.m-w.com), and Wikipedia (https://en.wikipedia.org).
2. Wikipedia, "Emotion."
3. Ibid., citing Steven J. C. Gaulin and Donald H. McBurney, *Evolutionary Psychology* (Prentice Hall, 2003), 121–142.
4. S. Chetty et al., "Stress and Glucocorticoids Promote Oligodendrogenesis in the Adult Hippocampus," *Molecular Psychiatry* 19 (December 2014): 1275–83; B. S. McEwen, "Physiology and Neurobiology of Stress and Adaptation: Central Role of the Brain," *Physiological Reviews* 87, no. 3 (July 2007): 873–904.
5. See "No Time to Be Nice at Work," http://mobile.nytimes.com/2015/06/21/opinion/sunday/is-your-boss-mean.html?referrer=.
6. http://www.nytimes.com/2015/04/12/education/edlife/how-to-be-emotionally-intelligent.html?smprod=nytcore-iphone&smid=nytcore-iphone-share.

Chapter 3

1. Steve Jobs, presentation of the "Think Different" marketing campaign, 1997, https://www.youtube.com/watch?v=dR-ZT8mhfJ4.
2. Tom Kolditz, "Why You Lead Determines How Well You Lead," *Harvard Business Review*, July 22, 2014.
3. Speech to students at Stanford, https://www.youtube.com/watch?v=zkTf0LmDqKI.

Chapter 4

1. Tom Peters, "What's Culture Got to Do with It?" http://tompeters.com/2007/02/whats-culture-got-to-do-with-it/.

Chapter 5

1. TED Talk, "The Power of Vulnerability," https://www.ted.com/talks/brene_brown_on_vulnerability?language=en.
2. The Best Way for New Leaders to Build Trust, *Harvard Business Review*, December 13, 2013.
3. Interview by Fareed Zakaria, CNN, 2010, http://transcripts.cnn.com/TRANSCRIPTS/1012/26/fzgps.02.html.

4. John Sadowsky, *Las Siete Reglas del Storytelling* (Buenos Aires, México, Montevideo y Santiago: Ediciones Granica, 2013).
5. http://www.strategy-business.com/article/10279?gko=abf36.

Chapter 6

1. *HBR's 10 Must Reads on Leadership* and *Leader to Leader: Enduring Insights on Leadership*, volumes 1 and 2, edited by Frances Hesselbein and Alan Shrader. Decision making is not once mentioned in any of the three tables of contents.
2. Zappos Family Core Values. Zappos.com.
3. Steve Jobs, WWDC, 1997, https://www.youtube.com/watch?v=FF-tKLISfPE#t=285.
4. http://quotations.about.com/od/stillmorefamouspeople/a/SamWalton1.htm.
5. Antonio Damasio, *When Emotions Make Better Decisions*, FORA .tv, https://www.youtube.com/watch?v=1wup_K2WN0I.

Chapter 7

1. Steve Ballmer at Stanford University, https://www.youtube.com/watch?v=W-BdCpZjZxU.
2. Daniel Roberts, "Carlos Brito: (Brew)master of the Universe," *Forbes*, August 15, 2013.
3. Ed Catmull, "How Pixar Fosters Collective Creativity," *Harvard Business Review*, September 1, 2008.
4. William C. Taylor and Polly LaBarre, "How Pixar Adds a New School of Thought to Disney," *New York Times*, January 29, 2006.
5. Catmull, "How Pixar Fosters Collective Creativity."
6. https://en.wikipedia.org/wiki/Ledesma_S.A.A.I.

Chapter 8

1. Rik Kirkland, "Leading in the 21st Century: An Interview with Carlos Ghosn," *McKinsey Quarterly*, September 2012, http://www.mckinsey.com/global-themes/leadership/an-interview-with-carlos-ghosn.
2. Pablo Hacker, "La Conexion Argentina de Guardiola," *La Nacion Canchallena*, http://canchallena.lanacion.com.ar/1459857-la-conexion-argentina-de-guardiola.
3. http://www.razonyfe.org/images/stories/Entrevista_al_papa_Francisco.pdf; http://www.laiglesiaenlaprensa.com/2013/09/

la-entrevista-del-papa-francisco-a-la-civilt%C3%A0-cattolica
-aqu%C3%AD-se-puede-descargar-el-ejemplar-original-en-pdf
-aqu%C3%AD-una.html.

4. Elisabetta Piqué, *Francisco: Vida y Revolución* (Argentina: El Ateneo, 2013).

5. Ibid.

6. Ibid.

Acknowledgments

Because this book is the work of a lifetime, it is impossible to thank all those who have made it possible. That said, I do wish to thank those who were more directly involved in bringing it into existence: the people I worked with at the HSM Group, who contributed to my growth—particularly Jose Salibi Neto, who helped me become passionate about the study of management and leadership and with whom I had the pleasure of conversing and building relationships with the finest global leaders. Leonardo Taffur, who contributed to finishing the first version of this text; and David Kammerman, who worked hand-in-hand with me to rewrite the book so that it became a more appealing story to the reader. Additionally, I would like to thank all the leaders worldwide who shared their knowledge and insights with me— explicitly or implicitly, whether they are quoted in this book or not—and who graciously allowed me to interpret and now share that knowledge and those insights with you. In particular, I wish to thank Jack Welch, who was the first to open my eyes to a new reality of the importance of people in business, and who is my mentor and friend. I thank my father, who was my first role model as a leader—and still is—and my mother, who taught me to listen beyond words. Finally, to all those who work tirelessly to build endeavors that are as human as the people that work in them, I offer my heartfelt gratitude and enduring encouragement.

Index